BEHIND THE SMILE

BEHIND THE SMILE

THE HIDDEN SIDE OF THE DALAI LAMA

MAXIME VIVAS

Translated from the French by
Lisa Molle Troyer

Long River Press
San Francisco

Published in the United States of America by
Sinomedia International Group
Long River Press
360 Swift Avenue, Suite 48
South San Francisco, CA 94080
www.longriverpress.com

ISBN 10: 1-59265-410-2
ISBN 13: 978-1-59265-140-5

To Frédéric, for his invaluable assistance

Contents

FOREWORD

"The Tibetan political regime before Chinese control was described by Western observers, when they discovered it in the 19th century, as a 'feudal theocracy.' Indeed, the political and economic organization of the country's traditional society was reminiscent of Europe in the Middle Ages, including its unified temporal and spiritual authority."[1]

"Outside the monasteries, our social system was feudal. There was inequality of wealth between the landed aristocracy at one extreme and the poorest peasants at the other."[2]

"[. . .] under the guidance of our religion, we shall

---

1. Translation of the report by the Franco-Tibetan friendship group to the French Senate on June 14, 2006.

2. Dalai Lama, *My Land and My People, The Original Autobiography of His Holiness the Dalai Lama of Tibet.* New York, McGraw-Hill, 1962.

[. . .] make a new Tibet, as happy in the modern world as old Tibet was in its isolation."[3]

Tibet. It is a harsh mountain region, dotted with monasteries and governed by serenity, brotherly love, spirituality, and harmony. It is also impoverished, stripped of its culture, and martyred by a genocidal colonial power (the fourteenth Dalai Lama has used the word *Holocaust*). This is the popular image of Tibet in a nutshell, an image so widely held in the Western world, that anyone daring to paint a different picture—or even add a hint of shading—is likely to become the target of a smear campaign.

I was in Tibet in July 2010 for the news commentary site *Le Grand Soir* (legrandsoir.info) as part of a group of journalists (representatives of French papers *Le Figaro* and *Le Monde*, plus two freelance reporters). At the start, I wasn't sure that my companions would see the same thing as me. As Seneca said, "*Why do you wonder that globe-trotting does not help you, seeing that you always take yourself with you?*" No doubt he was right; how can we avoid slipping into our luggage a bit of what we are and the medium we use to express ourselves? Reading each other's work after our return, it became clear that while we had "taken ourselves" along, our eyes were still open. We each reported objective facts to our respective readers, although that didn't prevent us from adding in our own subjective opinions.

---

3. *Ibid.*

Each journalist certainly could have chosen to write about the central authority in Beijing, dig through the archives about Tibet's past and imagine its ideal future. But after noticing that the shop signs, street names and signposts were written in Tibetan (and then in Mandarin), as were the newspapers; observing Tibetan-language radio and television; and visiting a university where the students and their professors had developed software in Tibetan, no one could possibly trot out the old refrain of cultural genocide. And so no one tried. In fact, our regional cultures back home would probably love to try that kind of persecution, especially since the Tibetan language is also compulsory from the beginning of elementary school through middle school (high school is taught in Mandarin and English).

In short, despite our differences, which happily demonstrate that France is open to divergent ways of thinking, there remained a common core of things we had seen together at the same time. These things are the truth, even if they have never been written about by the Dalai Lama's admirers or covered in the media by journalists who read each other's work and practice what Pierre Bourdieu called the "circular circulation of information."

"Listen, friend," the old backpacker may whisper to the naïve new arrival, "Don't forget to say that things aren't perfect in Tibet and that the current system would never suit the French." Certainly, the French constitution contains a few good clauses that would be helpful in Lhasa, the Tibetan capital, and in the Himalayan hill station of

Dharamsala, seat of the Dalai Lama's government-in-exile in India. Incidentally, they go beyond the strict separation of church and state or the conspicuous occupation of public space by a single faith.

As for Tibet's race toward modernism—with improved living standards, subsidized economic sectors, newly-built schools and hospitals, a growing use of solar power, preserved natural resources, the conservation of sacred texts, a flourishing culture, respect for local customs, restored monasteries, and the freedom to practice Buddhism in the temples and streets—none of the journalists I traveled with (whose opinions cover a broad political spectrum) wrote a single line to the effect that it is pure communist propaganda. Their criticism was aimed elsewhere.

So I will be talking about things that we saw together, and that I would be shocked to hear any of my four colleagues, despite our different approaches, describe as the product of my biased imagination.

Readers may be wondering about all these disclaimers. The reason is simple: in France, it is considered perfectly polite to argue over the past of the Catholic Church and the Pope, including his choices, forced or unforced, as a teenager in Nazi Germany; to debate our sudden obsession with Islam after the September 11 attacks in New York; or to discuss Judaism, which was persecuted in Europe and in whose name we shattered and divided Palestine. But woe unto he who questions the sacred cow of Tibet and the fourteenth Dalai Lama, media darling and Nobel Peace Prize winner, who is as untouchable as Mahatma Gandhi, priest and homeless campaigner Abbé Pierre, Desmond Tutu, Nelson Mandela or Martin Luther King, Jr.—men to whom the Dalai Lama's champions have erroneously compared him.

The Greek sages might have asked, "Where do you come from?" inviting us to consider the interests and motives of the people we encounter. So, I tried to find out who backs the Dalai Lama and who are his most fervent supporters in France and other countries.

At a bookstore in Toulouse, I heard an old Spaniard's warning, "People only talk to convince others to agree with them," and then add mischievously, "Now I believe . . ." The same warning applies to this book. Nonetheless, most of its pages quote the Dalai Lama himself and those favorable to him, such as devotees of Tibet or Buddhism. I will also refer to reports on research excursions by members of French parliament, both left- and right-leaning, which add nuance to or contradict many articles of the pro-Dalai Lama propaganda in France.

Whenever critical information or opinions are supplied by others (sparingly), they have been cross-referenced and their sources will be cited so that readers can verify them. After all, we can hardly afford categorically to ignore those people around the world who have pulled back the Dalai Lama's deceptive mask: not only the Chinese authorities, but also their statisticians, economists, demographers and historians, whom I will not insult by claiming that nothing they say is true, especially when the facts they put forward can be independently verified and are confirmed by international entities and researchers from around the world.

1. THE UNTOUCHABLE

The Dalai Lama has two faces. The first wears an unwavering smile, projecting kindness, wisdom, tolerance, pacifism and inexhaustible patience in the face of persecution. This is the face that graces magazine covers and the countless books on Tibet that can be found in France and many other countries.

The second face bears the frown of a deposed monarch whose life is devoted to one supreme goal: returning to Lhasa to restore a theocratic authority that, although it can never be exactly the same as it once was, would essentially recreate the power he once enjoyed. The Dalai Lama inherited that power from his fearsome predecessors, and he was in no hurry to implement reforms eliminating the extraordinary institutional violence that had been stamped out by the civilized world centuries before.

Around the world, there is suffering from high unemployment, job security is waning, families are being broken apart, many fear for the future, companies have been faced with a string of suicides and many countries in the Western world are the heaviest consumers of antidepressants.

In parallel, we are witnessing the decline of France's largest religion: the churches are emptying out. In the countryside, several parishes often share a single priest. People marry less often, go to confession rarely and make stingy contributions to the collection plate and parish costs. Faith is in crisis, the Vatican recommendations are being criticized and papal infallibility rejected, while more and more questions surround the dogma that once eased evangelization. The cloven-hoofed devil has disappeared from sermons, God is no longer seated on a cloud, the story that Eve was created from part of Adam's body could be the result of a bad translation, and so on. Heaven is becoming an increasingly blurred concept, since people are no longer attracted by the promise that spending time in houses of worship can make a soul live forever.

Almost hourly, the media report on the new god to whom we should all genuflect, in temples of electronics called "stock markets" adorned with lights, honoring modern saints with barbaric names like CAC 40, Dow Jones, and NASDAQ.

Still, materialism has never been enough to provide fulfillment in a human life. Each of us harbors some vestige of spirituality, or dreams if you prefer; the hope of something intangible and benevolent.

And it does transfer. When belief declines in one arena, eroded by the history of a Church devoted to riches, armies and the mighty, and guilty of a thousand crimes, we seek it elsewhere, in a religion that to us is unsullied, with new rites, dressed up in the virtues of love for one's neighbor, capable of bestowing an unhoped-for inner calm or even protecting our health. This new religion speaks in deliciously exotic words; its monasteries, redolent of yak butter candles, are thronged with priests in saffron robes and home to immense Buddhas who gleam in their gold leaf. It is a religion whose Mecca is the "Roof of the World," a religion symbolized by the perpetual public smile plastered urbi et orbi over the face of a living, nomadic icon, a sort of international Care Bear for grown-ups. Seen in this light, it is easy to see how the Dalai Lama's Buddhism could win over not only the bohemian chic of Paris or the hippie population (although they were the first to actively convert), but anyone seeking a little spirituality, happiness, or just something new.

The problem is that in this case, the intrinsic virtues of Buddhism serve as a screen for men whose priorities are their flesh and blood, appetites and ambitions, and their nostalgia for lost power and an era of stagnant adversity that they romanticize, as we will see shortly.

Buddhism. I called it a "religion," but without a revealed god, is it not better described as a creator of worlds, a philosophy, or a spiritual belief? That simple question can stir up clouds of controversy. The Dalai Lama, who is living proof of the soul's immortality, cannot start out as just anyone. He is a reincarnation of himself (and can apparently prove it at the age of four), and this justifies his claim of spiritual and temporal leadership over a vast territory whose inhabitants belong to his flock. They also call him

His Holiness, prostrate themselves before him as others do before the Pope and venerate effigies of his predecessors (his own are forbidden in China), alongside Buddhas, in temples where candles burn in front of altars. With monasteries, a liturgy, monks, worship, sacred texts, chants, acts of devotion, prayer wheels, prayer flags and the promise of life after death, it certainly looks like a religion. It even offers a philosophy and a set of "self-help" tools for the uninitiated. The Dalai Lama uses the word "religion," however, and so I will do the same, even though I realize it may sound simplistic to readers who seek (and have perhaps found) something else in Buddhism.

In any event, if Buddhism is just a philosophy, it is the only one in the world today to dress itself up in such finery, require so many rituals and acknowledge a master who intends in its name to lead a vast territory which banishes all other philosophies—and even its own followers, if they deviate by so much as an inch.

This book does not aim to challenge a particular style of worship or the Chinese political system. Plenty of others have already addressed those topics, and I have chosen to tackle a different one: the Dalai Lama himself. Although he is the spiritual master of a mere handful of the world's hundreds of millions of Buddhists, the media's power has somehow made him appear to be the religion's sole pope. He also aspires to be the all-powerful leader of a territory one-third the size of the United States, which occupies a quarter of China's land, where the entire law will follow from the Dharma (the Universal Law of Nature according to Buddhism), i.e. religious texts.

The question is, what would a "free Tibet" look like under the leadership of a prophet who seems oddly forgetful about the horrors of Nazism, who grumbles at science[4] and still mourns for the highlands over which he once ruled, despite being blind to its anachronisms?

Would democracy in China benefit, and would the world be a better place for it?

Also, is the media and humanitarian furor surrounding Tibet simply an attempt to trigger China's own version of the Ukrainian Orange Revolution, which was supervised and funded from abroad and shook the country to its core in 2004 to serve the geopolitical interests of the American empire?

We will try to answer these questions through a rational analysis that relies mainly, as I have said, on irrefutable texts, almost all of them taken from the Dalai Lama himself, his accomplices, or friendly observers.

"Respected the world over and welcomed by heads of state, the man with the saffron robe and the infectious laugh still embodies the hopes of six million Tibetans living in Tibet and in exile," stated an AFP dispatch dated November 22, 2008.

France 24, however, an international news channel that styles itself the "French CNN," is less sanguine about

---

4. See chapter II.

the Dalai Lama's kindly authority over all of Chinese Buddhism. On August 9, 2009, the channel's *Reporters* news program broadcast a story by Capucine Henry and Nicolas Haque.

Viewers were alarmed to see the Dalai Lama giving "a speech of rare violence in a South Indian university" on January 7, 2008. This Dalai Lama was a frightening specter as he enjoined his exiled flock not to speak to their brothers and sisters who practice Shugden.

Shugden is a deity in the Buddhist tradition who is venerated in most parts of the world, including China, India, Nepal, Mongolia, Bhutan and Bangladesh, not to mention Russia, Europe and the United States.

On August 12, 2005 in Zurich, the Dalai Lama had already publicly declared his hostility to a faith that no longer suited him: "Some of you might know, some not, that in the Tibetan tradition there is a practice of a deity who is called Dorje Shugden, that some are following this practice, practicing veneration of this deity, and that I am against this practice because it goes against my principles and those of the Dalai Lamas."

France 24 explained the procedure behind the exiled sage's decision to "firmly condemn the Shugden movement and its followers." Meanwhile, admirers of the self-proclaimed global spokesman for a gentle, Zen-like democracy, unlike the Chinese political system, listened in dismay to the autocratic views of His Holiness: "I have not decided to put aside Shugden in my own interest; I have meditated and considered my decision at length in my soul and spirit."[5]

This blacklisting had concrete effects: accomplices of His Holiness spoke out in the street to condemn their brothers and sisters, who began to suffer serious discrimination in their daily lives. Public notices informed them that they were no longer welcome in certain places. According to one Tibetan living in a village in South India, every door was closed to him and the other members of his community. In just a few months, these deviants had been banished by a community that is generally assumed to be welcoming because it is Buddhist. France 24 drove home the point: "The Shugden monks can no longer enter stores, public spaces or even hospitals. In the streets, you can see portraits of their leaders posted on walls, like outlaws."

It is all too easy to make facile comparisons as an excuse for overturning a long-standing assumption. Yet what are we to think when a designated minority is banned from stores and denounced on posters that feature photographs of men who were once our brothers, but now the enemy?

The last straw is that the Dalai Lama himself practiced this form of worship before he began to advise against it, then forbade it and finally decided to clap irons onto anyone who remained faithful to it, thereby becoming agents of Beijing in his eyes. So accused, they were reduced to pariahs in India, a country where the Dalai Lama does not

5. France 24, previously cited program.

even officially write the law. Might we extrapolate the fate that would have awaited Shugden practitioners in a Tibet ruled over by the Dalai Lama and his own? And what about the global outcry that would inevitably follow any attempt by the Beijing government to take the same measures in Tibet against the branch of Buddhism led by the Dalai Lama?

Once the excommunication was complete, the propaganda had only to justify it. The Dalai Lama had made the decision alone, but his followers were now forced to join in the demonization. In Dharamsala, India, the Prime Minister explained that "first and foremost, Shugden practitioners are political enemies, domestic enemies." One of their number, a very influential man, was guilty of terrible crimes: he "has visited China at least two or three times." The official position was clear: "They're willing to kill anyone, to strike anyone," he continued. So the Shugden were murderers and worse, traitors on the Chinese payroll, according to those close to the Dalai Lama. "The Shugden and the Chinese are linked, that much is clear," continued the Prime Minister. "All those who practice Shugden are financed by the Chinese."[6]

This unsubstantiated accusation was not without irony, coming from the close allies of a Dalai Lama who, rather indiscreetly, received funding from the United States Central Intelligence Agency for decades.[7]

In 2003, Kelsang Gyaltsen, envoy of the 14th Dalai

---

6. *Ibid.*
7. See chapter VI.

Lama to the European Union, affirmed that the religious leader was favorable to the separation of church and state and had decided no longer to hold a post in the Tibetan administration after returning to Tibet. That would have been excellent news, if only his current decisions did not prove that his meditative subconscious in India is still guided by the way he and his predecessors once governed Tibet.

This is a sort of double-speak. In August 2011, when he visited Toulouse in the south of France, the Dalai Lama had an informational document published whose paragraph on *Promoting inter-religious harmony* offers these excellent thoughts: "[. . .] on the level of a religious practitioner, His Holiness' second commitment is the promotion of religious harmony and understanding among the world's major religious traditions. Despite philosophical differences, all major world religions have the same potential to create good human beings. It is therefore important for all religious traditions to respect one another and recognize the value of each other's respective traditions. As far as one truth/one religion is concerned, this is relevant on an individual level. However, for the community at large, several truths/several religions are necessary."[8]

Words are a good start. Now he simply has to avoid going back into his kingdom, with a black look, pointed finger and lofty tone, and doing exactly the opposite of what he murmurs outside its borders with a low bow, hands joined, and a malicious smile lighting up his face.

---

8. http://www.dalailama-toulouse2011.fr/EN/ssdl_engagements.php

Far from being "respected the world over," the Dalai Lama, who represents one of the four branches of Buddhism in Tibet (the Yellow Hats) and two percent of the world's Buddhists, is now being challenged even by some of those who followed him into exile. Since, as we will see, the Dalai Lama scorns the 55 other ethnic groups that make up China, his only legitimate claim to near-unanimous support is from the Western media; by warming up and (de)forming public opinion, even political demagogues bow devotedly before him.

Yet somehow, this devotion never goes so far as to follow the Dalai Lama in claiming independence for Tibet. All of the UN member states (not all of whom are friends with China or pleased at its growing power) recognize Tibet as a region of China and not one nation occupied by another. In January 2011, when he received Chinese President Hu Jintao in Washington, U.S. President Barack Obama reaffirmed that "the United States recognizes Tibet as part of the People's Republic of China." In other words, not a single country goes along with the Dalai Lama's demands for Tibetan independence. No one advocates putting the idea to a vote in the region. Constitutions of some Western nations describe their countries as "one" and "indivisible" and offer no mechanism for a regional or national referendum that would splinter the country. As such, it would be an ill-advised move to encourage such a precedent elsewhere.

Given these conditions, why should the West, whose memories of World War II are still painfully fresh, wish for China to be subdivided in favor of a man who seems strangely forgetful where Nazism is concerned? On September 10, 2006, free thinker Georges-André Morin declared, "It is staggering to think that in 1994, the current Dalai Lama wanted to convene a meeting in London of key Western figures who had known Tibet as independent. The seven guests included two Waffen SS members—mountaineer Heinrich Harrer and Auschwitz anthropologist Bruno Beger—and a Chilean diplomat by the name of Miguel Serrano who built his career in the footsteps of Kurt Waldheim, forming close relationships with Augusto Pinochet and the Nazi communities in southern Chile." In April 1999, the Dalai Lama appealed to the British government to free Pinochet, who was arrested while visiting England.

Laurent Dispot addressed the same topic in the daily paper *Libération*, writing that Harrer joined the Sturmabteilung (SA) in 1933 when Hitler took power, and that he later moved into the SS and was "a favorite of Reichsführer Heinrich Himmler." "He was entrusted with a mission by Hitler and Himmler themselves: infiltrate Tibet, with the approval of the young Dalai Lama's regents, to become the child's private tutor."[9] Harrer's lackeys insist that, because he was not in Europe during the Second World War, he did not participate in the atrocities committed by the SS. That is true. Instead, he accomplished a mission "with mystical, racist and strategic motives," searching for pure races. He

---

9. Translation of Dispot, Laurent, "Le dalaï-lama et l'honneur nazi." *Libération*, April 25, 2008.

spent the remainder of his life attempting to hide his Nazi past, preferring to extol the virtues of a Tibet he saw as the "gold standard for a clerical dictatorship."

The Dalai Lama has scrubbed his childhood of this episode. His own version seems to suggest that the thick walls of the Potala Palace monastery blocked out the tumult of World War II. At most, he heard "accounts" of it. "But few world events affected us in Lhasa."[10] Apparently SS member Harrer never mentioned it . . . In any event, the sage has never distanced himself from this peculiar tutor who was sent to him on an assignment for the Führer. On the contrary, he still thanks the man who "introduced him to the West and to modernity."[11]

Equally troubling are the Dalai Lama's ties to Shoko Asahara, founder of the Japanese religious group Aum Shinrikyo and sponsor of the Tibet cause (photos show the two men hand in hand). This same Asahara horrified the world with a sarin gas attack on Tokyo subway passengers on March 20, 1995.

The final unsettling detail, as we will see, is his relationship with the CIA.

There is clearly reason to lament the fact that, in his struggle for independence, the Dalai Lama has had so little concern for the methods he uses or his choice of allies, friends and funders.

---

10. Dalai Lama, *op. cit.*, p. 35.
11. Dispot, Laurent, *op. cit.*

2. AN IMMOVABLE REIGN

"For a long time already you have tried to put a gag on the human intellect [. . .]. You wish to be the masters of education. [. . .] If the mind of humanity were there before your eyes, at your discretion, open as the page of a book, you would censure it [. . .]"[12]

"During my education, I learned very little of any other social system but our own [. . .]"[13]

Lhamo Dhondrub was born on July 6, 1935 in Takster, a village in the Amdo province at an elevation of 9,300 feet. Later, the village would become Hongya in the Chinese province of Qinghai.

At the age of two, the child showed "evidence" of be-

12. Hugo, Victor, quoted in "Report upon public schools and education, in the state of Rhode Island." Rhode Island Commissioner of Public Schools, Elisha Reynolds Potter, pp. 73-74.

13. Dalai Lama, *op. cit.*

ing the reincarnation of the 13th Dalai Lama. Rational minds may express their skepticism, but since that claim is not the subject of this work, we will not comment further. Likewise, we will allow his mother to maintain that at the age of two, the child, whose native tongue was the Xining dialect of Chinese, began spontaneously to speak Lhasa Tibetan, the language of his predecessor. The Dalai Lama himself has taken care not to confirm this excessively far-fetched legend.

Lhamo Dhondrub was selected as the 14th Dalai Lama with the name Jetsun Jamphel Ngawang Lobsang Yeshe Tenzin Gyatso, which translates to "Holy Lord, Gentle Glory, Compassionate, Defender of the Faith, Ocean of Wisdom." He is not averse to being called simply Yeshe Norbu ("Wish-Fulfilling Jewel").

He began his monastic education at the age of six. In 1950, still only 15 years old, he was enthroned as the spiritual and temporal leader of Tibet.

The 14th Dalai Lama therefore ruled for nine years, from 1950 to 1959 (when he fled to India). During that time, along with his regent and advisors, he consented to practices in which religious freedom, freedom for women (those convicted of adultery had their nose and ears slit), freedom for peasants, in short, freedom in general and compassion for the people were no more prevalent (and quite probably less) than they were in the Middle Ages. In his Autobiography, he explains that he was getting ready to introduce reforms just as the Chinese army entered Tibet.

By acting so inexcusably slowly, he allowed the central government in Beijing to abolish slavery and serfdom, do away with corvée labor and private religious justice, establish schools, teach the people to read and write, stimulate demographic growth when it had been stagnant for two centuries, and nearly double life expectancy for Tibet's citizens.

Slavery has been prohibited since 1926 by the Geneva Convention, since 1930 by the International Labor Organization (ILO) and since 1948 by the Universal Declaration of Human Rights, whose fourth article states, "No one shall be held in slavery or servitude; slavery and the slave trade shall be prohibited in all their forms."

The 14th Dalai Lama, last of a long line in power, fled to India on March 17, 1959. On March 28, 11 days later, serfdom and slavery were abolished in Tibet (neighboring countries where monks did not write the law had already done the same, much earlier: 1923 in Afghanistan and 1956 in Bhutan). The measure benefited nearly a million Tibetans, that is, the 95% of the population who were not among it's masters: aristocrats, monks and living Buddhas.

In Tibet under the Dalai Lamas, the domination by monks was so harsh that, apparently, it is best not even to mention it and to quibble over words when others expose its abuses. For example, there is a controversy over whether or not slavery and serfdom really existed. Let us refer to the definition adopted in 1956 to supplement the Geneva Convention of 1926, and more specifically to the "Supplementary Convention on the Abolition of Slavery, the Slave

Trade, and Institutions and Practices Similar to Slavery." It defines serfdom as follows:

"Serfdom, that is to say, the condition or status of a tenant who is by law, custom or agreement bound to live and labour on land belonging to another person and to render some determinate service to such other person, whether for reward or not, and is not free to change his status."

Were the destitute of Tibet not under such constraints? The Dalai Lama himself, in his *Autobiography*, made no such claim—on the contrary. As for slavery, the convention defines it as "the status or condition of a person over whom any or all of the powers attaching to the right of ownership are exercised."

Alexandra David-Néel was a great explorer and an uncontested specialist on and friend of Tibet. She was received in Dharamsala by the Dalai Lama and, after her death, he traveled twice (in October 1982 and May 1986) to the home where she was born in Digne, France. He publicly commended her for introducing Tibetan culture to Westerners. In her book *Grand Tibet et vaste Chine*, she concedes, "A sort of benign slavery still exists in many parts of Tibet."[14] Dalai Lama supporters determined to deny this fact quibble over certain freedoms that were granted to the poor, apparently raising them from the status of slaves.

Tibetan law under the Dalai Lamas, however, bears a striking resemblance to a French text from 1685, namely

---

14. Translation of David-Néel, Alexandra, *Grand Tibet et vaste Chine*. Paris, Omnibus 1994, republished 1999, p. 985.

Colbert's "Code Noir." This edict of the king on his policy for the islands of French America was officially aimed at providing legal protection for slaves. In both the royalist France of long ago and the former theocratic Tibet, masters had the right to punish their people, force them to practice a religion, sanction runaways and thieves, have them put in chains, whipped, imprisoned or amputated, put them to death and grant or refuse permission to marry. Any who dared raise a hand against their master risked a palette of punishments that varied with the severity of the infraction and the importance of its target. Only someone with a truly black sense of humor could see the same laws that described slavery in our own case as only a harmless sort of sharecropping in Tibet.

In short, it took 17 years of professional training plus nine years of rule for the Dalai Lama to cunningly announce his desire, imposed by his kindness and love for democracy, to eventually put an end to the feudal legacy that showered power and riches on 14 Dalai Lamas and their inner circle.

Of course, many readers will rightfully have a great deal to say about the Chinese version of democracy and the system that currently holds sway in Lhasa. But I suspect that they will object even more strenuously to discovering what the Dalai Lama's government really was, as well as the aims of the Tibetan government-in-exile.

In 1963, the John Didier publishing house in Paris printed *Mémoirs du dalaï-lama* with a possessive subtitle,

Ma terre et mon peuple. The work was initially published in the United States as *My Land and My People*, in 1962. At the time, the author was 27 years old, and he prefaced the French edition with a "Message to French readers" in which he hoped that the book would help them "get to know [his] country better."

In fact, readers ended up getting to know the Dalai Lama himself while reading the book, which demonstrates both a certain political naïveté and an early talent for evasion, along with acceptance for a situation he not only does not consider an anachronism, but also claims is a source of happiness for all Tibetans (even those who do not recognize his authority are lumped together in his account): "Thus, when I was four-and-a-half years old, I was formally recognized as the 14th Dalai Lama, the spiritual and temporal ruler of Tibet. To all Tibetans, the future seemed happy and secure."[15]

As we can see, it is stated right from the start that the Dalai Lama does not share his rule, and that he has religious and political authority over the three branches of Buddhism that do not recognize him.

He then attempts to justify a theocracy that is fixed over time, rejects external progress and remains closed to contributions by visitors from the outside. Seeking a euphemism, the Dalai Lama finds and systematically repeats the word *isolation*. In addition to the physical distance that

---

15. Dalai Lama, *op. cit.* p. 21

makes Tibet so hard to reach, this refers to a watertight cultural, scientific, ideological and xenophobic edifice that rejects the same knowledge that previously enlightened most of the world's other peoples, except possibly for a few primitive tribes who were hidden away deep in the forest and discovered only later. Those rare Tibetans who were able to go to school were force-fed Buddhism, while the modern sciences were not taught at all. This wholesale boycott of the same knowledge that pulled the rest of the world up out of its miserable ancestral conditions has created a massive delay: even today, half a century after school was made compulsory, Tibetan students are given bonus points on their grades (positive discrimination) to bring their pass rates in line with the other Chinese students.

So what exactly constituted education under "the traditional system of Tibet"? The Dalai Lama assigns it many virtues, even as he recognizes that it "has the defect of entirely ignoring the scientific knowledge of recent centuries, but the reason for that, of course, is that Tibet remained entirely isolated until very recent times."[16] Despite the tortuous turn of phrase, he seems to be hinting that Tibet was closed off and the sciences banned until Beijing put an end to these defects by filling the vacant seat of authority with its own administration.

Up to that time, what type of education was dispensed to the Tibetans—or more precisely, to the five percent

---

16. *Ibid.*, p. 22.

of them who received it? First, the "five minor subjects," namely "drama, dance and music, astrology, poetry and composition." And did they study all five?

No, pupils receiving religious education could choose simply to study "astrology and composition."[17]

Next, the "five higher subjects" of higher education, which are "the art of healing, Sanskrit, dialectics, arts and crafts, and metaphysics and the philosophy of religion [of which] the last is the most important and fundamental."[18] These can be further subdivided into five parts: the Perfection of Wisdom, the Middle Path, the Canon of Monastic Discipline, Metaphysics, and Logic and Dialectics.

Though neatly formatted, Tibet's scholars were barely more aware than the average illiterate serf of the knowledge that has enriched the world's thinking and intelligence for centuries while improving daily life. Physics, chemistry, mechanics, architecture, economics, philosophical or artistic movements and other impious trivialities were blocked from entering into mystical Tibet by a deliberate policy of "isolation." No one knew or was supposed to know about such topics as geometry and algebra, let alone teach them, although these heresies were considered useful everywhere else for centuries before our own time.

Naturally, world history and geography were not any more welcome; they were seen as disciplines unlikely to help perpetuate the theocracy and potentially even danger-

17. *Ibid.*
18. *Ibid.*

ous. Poring over the descriptions of distant countries in an atlas, the future leader of Tibet observed that he "did not know anyone who had ever seen them."[19] "I grew up with hardly any knowledge of worldly affairs, and it was in that state, when I was sixteen, that I was called upon to lead my country against the invasion of Communist China."[20]

The ruling class was eager to promote the intentional, organized ignorance that protected the status quo, an ignorance without which the "proud, courageous and warlike" Tibetan people, as the Dalai Lama himself describes them, would probably have shaken off the yoke of religious oppression, which had no parallel in the world when the religious leader ascended to power. The Tibetans were the orphans of this revolt, which spared their monks but stripped them of their temporal power, eliminated the parasitic aristocracy yet left the common people caught in a net on every side, deprived of knowledge, modernity, democratic rights, non-religious justice and permission to travel or entertain foreigners.

"Perhaps the best-known quality of Tibet in the recent past was its deliberate isolation. [. . .] We increased our natural isolation by allowing the fewest possible foreigners into our country."[21]

"Most people in the distant marches of Tibet had never been to Lhasa, or even perhaps met anyone else who had

---

19. *Ibid.*, p. 35.
20. *Ibid.*, p. 36.
21. *Ibid.*, p. 38.

been there. From year to year they tilled the earth and bred their yaks and other animals, and neither heard nor saw what happened in the world beyond their own horizon."[22]

Besides, how could these poor souls have traveled, without a penny to their name, forced to work interminably long days and perform corvée labor for the nobles and monks (as many as two hundred corvée obligations have been counted)? And how could they afford the risk of leaving their land and giving the impression that they had run away, a crime punished with unimaginable cruelty? According to Tibetologist Wang Gui, who lived and worked in Tibet from 1950 to 1981, in segments broadcast on China Radio International, "The serfs were beaten down by three hammers: corvée labor, taxes, and excessively high interest on loans. Peasants had three options: flight, slavery or begging."[23]

Two Americans visiting Tibet in the 1960s interviewed a former serf, Tsereh Wang Tuei, who had once stolen two sheep belonging to a monastery. As punishment, his eyes were gouged out and his hand mutilated. He is no longer Buddhist.[24]

Terror, combined with isolation, propped up an appallingly unjust political system that could have been shaken by the revelation of other foreign systems that had

---

22. *Ibid.*, p. 42.

23. Translation of "Tibet. L'émancipation des serfs, 'grande victoire des droits de l'homme', jugent des experts." CRI Online, March 18, 2009.

24. Stuart and Roma Gelder, *The Timely Rain: Travels in New Tibet*. New York, Monthly Review Press, 1964.

abolished the savage practices still in effect in Tibet. "During my education, I learned very little of any other social system but our own. Tibetans in general, I think, regarded it as the natural state of affairs [. . .],"[25] admitted the Dalai Lama naïvely.

No doubt they also saw the massive population of monks and nuns as natural: "There are no exact figures, but probably ten per cent of the total population were monks or nuns."[26] This figure may even be slightly low; the Chinese authorities talk of 125,000 monks in a population of one million at the time, which would be more than 12 percent of the total population. It is safe to say that some 25 percent of the male population was kept out of the workforce and the gene pool.

Surrounded by hordes of monks and worked to the bone to feed and clothe them, unaware of another world that operated differently, savagely put down if ever they disobeyed yet consoled before their deaths (around age 35, on average) by the belief that, thanks to their suffering, they would be reincarnated into an idyllic life, the Tibetans never revolted. From this point of view, regardless of one's personal opinion of Maoist China and the Cultural Revolution that tried to tear down every vestige of the past (leaving all the monasteries marked out for Tibetan or Han members of the Red Guards), whatever reservations one might have about modern China and its regional

25. Dalai Lama, *op. cit.*, p. 43.
26. *Ibid.*, p. 39.

policies, there can be no doubt that Beijing brought the light to Lhasa. The Chinese authorities transformed what Tibet's masters called "talking animals" into citizens with the same rights as any other Chinese, and while there is no doubt that those rights could afford to be extended further, even they had been previously denied to 95 percent[27] of Tibetans.

Injustice ruled in the monasteries as well. Poor young monks were ripped away from their parents at a very young age to act as domestic servants for the others. And as for the nobility, they were very skilled at identifying pretty girls who would make good "personal servants."

"It is often said by people of other religions that belief in rebirth—the law of karma—tends to make people accept inequalities of fortune, perhaps too readily. This is only partly true. A poor Tibetan peasant was less inclined to envy or resent his rich Tibetan landlord, because he knew that each of them was reaping the seed he had sown in his previous life. [. . .] In this light, Tibetans accepted our social system without any question."[28]

And they not only accepted their lot uncomplainingly; they were, to put it ironically, in seventh heaven: "Yet with all the faults of its [social] system, and the rigor of

27. "Démographie Tibet. Rétrospective sur le développement économique et social des cinquante dernières années." *GéoPopulation*, Xinhua, March 30, 2009. French article at http://www.geopopulation.com/20090331/demographie-tibet-retrospective-sur-le-developpement-economique-et-social-des-50-dernieres-annees/.

28. Dalai Lama, *op. cit.*, p. 46.

its climate, I am sure that Tibet was among the happiest of lands." "So we were happy." "[By] my dual position as Dalai Lama, Tibet had been happily ruled for centuries,"[29] especially since, "feudal though the system was, it was different from any other feudal system, because at the apex of it was the incarnation of Chenresi, a being whom all the people, for hundreds of years, had regarded with the highest reverence."[30]

Happy people living in Shangri-La, an earthly paradise: it all sounds strangely like a self-hypnosis script or an advertising scheme. In January 2005, during his second inaugural address, U.S. President George W. Bush pronounced the words *freedom* and *liberty* a total of forty times, averaging once every thirty seconds. Meanwhile, the Dalai Lama managed to say *happiness* 12 times in *A Human Approach to World Peace*.[31]

In actuality, under the leadership of the Dalai Lamas, there was no happiness for Tibetans being punished in this life for their faults in a previous one, yet destined for a glorious future life if they accept this one selflessly.

Securely gripping the steel bar of faith, his pincers are ready to bite *in secula seculorum* into the flesh of a confined and deluded people, dazed with fatigue, blinded by ignorance, dazzled by the magnificence of the monasteries,

---

29. *Ibid.*, p. 46, 47 and 108 respectively.
30. *Ibid.*, p. 47.
31. Dalai Lama, *A Human Approach to World Peace*. Wisdom Publications. Boston, 1984.

bowed down by the sheer size of the stern Buddha statues and drunk on prayers; a people convinced that Tibetan culture and its traditions are their cross to bear, and that any reform that might deliver them would be tantamount to sacrilege and add to the steep price they will have to pay in a future life, making it as hopeless as the one they must currently endure.

Meanwhile, the Potala Palace in Lhasa is "said to be one of the largest buildings in the world. Even after living in it for years, one could never know all its secrets. It entirely covers the top of a hill; it is a city in itself."[32] It "is thirteen stories high," and one can revel in "the mausoleums of seven Dalai Lamas—some 30 feet high and covered in solid gold and precious stones."[33]

Any one of its countless rooms may reveal a throng of monks, guards and servants, the Buddhist school, monks' apartments, or a prison "corresponding perhaps to the Tower of London"[34], and may be used to store thousands of pieces of jewelry and jade, satin garments, furs, coats set with pearls and precious stones, and tons of food. "Here were strong rooms filled with the golden regalia of the earliest kings of Tibet, dating back for a thousand years, and the sumptuous gifts they received from the Chinese or Mongol emperors, and the treasures of the Dalai Lamas who

32. Dalai Lama, *My Land and My People: The Original Autobiography of His Holiness the Dalai Lama of Tibet, op. cit.*, p. 31.

33. Dalai Lama, *op. cit.*, p. 32.

34. Dalai Lama, *op. cit.*, p. 33.

succeeded the kings."[35] "Down below the building there were endless underground storehouses and cellars, containing government stocks of butter, tea, and cloth which were supplied to the monasteries, the army, and government officials."[36]

Under the 13th Dalai Lama, European luxury products, fashionable clothing and imported perfumes began to arrive, facing little resistance but destined only for the rich.

Although the 14th Dalai Lama had no time during his brief reign to pick up a pen and sign a decree abolishing fatal injustices, corvée labor and slavery, practices that most (if not all) other religions had lived through and then discarded in other countries, it was still plenty long for him to expand his home during those "happier days."[37] Norbulingka was the summer palace of the Dalai Lamas, and they have "added their own residences to it ever since. I built one there myself."[38]

All around, the people who fed that lifestyle were dying young of fatigue, malnutrition, cold, disease and mistreatment, while Leaders and the rich drink heartily, but to the poor, he says, "friend, come and fast with me!"[39]

35. Dalai Lama, *op. cit.*, p. 32.
36. *Ibid.*, p. 33.
37. *Ibid.*, p. 37.
38. *Ibid.*, p. 34.
39. Hugo, Victor. *Les Châtiments* ("Castigations"). Paris, Gallimard, 1964.

3. THE ART OF THE SMILE

The People's Republic of China (PRC) was founded in October 1949. Its government operates under the supervision of the Communist Party of China. This is not breaking news; if anything, it is a piece of information that could distract us from the topic at hand. I mention it only to draw attention to the fact that for 10 years, the central Communist power and the Dalai Lama coexisted.

The 14th Dalai Lama has even held important posts within the Communist machine. In 1954, he was elected a vice-chairman of the Standing Committee of the National People's Congress. Mao Zedong personally assured him that no major reforms would be undertaken for six years in Tibet, whose identity was to be preserved.

The document published for the Dalai Lama's visit to Toulouse in August 2011 downplayed his position in the Chinese communist apparatus, stating simply, "In 1954 he traveled to Beijing in the hope of negotiating a peaceful settlement with Mao Zedong and other Chinese leaders, among them Zhou Enlai and Deng Xiaoping."

And yet in 1955, during the New Year's festivities in Beijing, the Dalai Lama gave a speech thanking the Chinese government and then wrote a poem to the glory of Mao. In 1956, he became chairman of the Preparatory Committee for the Tibet Autonomous Region (TAR). In November of the same year, he visited India to celebrate the 2,500th anniversary of Buddha's death. His two older brothers tried to convince him not to return to Tibet and instead to campaign for independence. To keep the Dalai Lama from opening hostilities, Zhou Enlai had to personally deliver a letter from Mao promising no changes in Tibet for the next six years.

Nevertheless, anxious to protect their privileges, the monks and aristocrats of Lhasa had already begun to stir up rebellion. In 1956, a revolt broke out in Litang and spread throughout the Kham region, reaching areas of the Kham region in 1957 and 1958, the Ü-Tsang region in 1958 and 1959, and the future Tibet Autonomous Region, finally arriving at Lhasa in March 1959. As we will see, the Dalai Lama played both sides and secretly instigated the unrest.

China is made up of 22 provinces, 5 autonomous regions, 30 autonomous prefectures and 124 autonomous counties, in addition to 1,300 ethnic townships in its multi-ethnic areas. Fragmentation is a constant risk in a country where some 200 languages (dialects) are spoken, including 24 Sinitic languages.

Having to govern and feed an immense, overpopulated country inhabited by 56 disparate ethnic groups while beating the drum for revolution in its social structures, Mao Zedong considered it prudent to postpone reforms in the Tibetan territory. Slavery, exploitation of the people by monks and nobles and the monolithic power of the Dalai Lama lasted for more than nine years in Communist China, even as the latter extolled the virtues of equality, education and technical and social advances against the backdrop of a Marxist philosophy that was hardly likely to consider religion all-powerful. The Chinese Communist Party, hoping to avoid bloody confrontations, sheathed its claws and coexisted with the world's last feudal theocracy, a system capable of refusing progress in any area.

In such times, the "isolation" of the Buddhist elite was no longer enough to keep them ignorant of events elsewhere in China and the rest of the world that, the world being what it is, might one day reach their own doorstep.

The destitute of Tibet, who whispered amongst themselves that they owned only their own shadows and would take only their dust with them when they died, had everything to gain from a more distributionist policy. But their masters—the nobles, monks and Dalai Lama—saw only that they were about to lose their privileges and, in the worst case, might have to answer for the past.

Under circumstances such as these, it is easy to see that the first shot against Beijing was already aimed and fired long before the uprising that forced the Dalai Lama to flee into India.

With his talent for double-speak, a surprising skill for

someone with his innocent reputation in the West, the Dalai Lama became the *deus ex machina* of the revolt, sitting in the highest state councils in Beijing, glorifying Mao and assuring him that he disowned the "reactionary criminals" and "groups of reactionaries," whose violence caused him "immense anxiety." He further insisted that he was doing "the impossible" to resolve the situation, and then that he had "taught a lesson to" and "harshly criticized" the rebels. No doubt many readers will want to cross-reference this information, which comes from a March 2009 publication by the State Council Information Office of the People's Republic of China. Let us see what the Dalai Lama himself says, in his *Autobiography,* about his communications with a Chinese general who was his contact in Lhasa: "I decided to reply in a way [that would seem] to accept his sympathy and welcome his advice. [. . .] I told him I had given orders that the people surrounding the Norbulingka should disperse."[40] All of this was said in letters "written to disguise my true intentions"[41] in an attempt to "seem to fall in with [the general's] wishes."[42] And so, as Lhasa itself teetered on the point of a violent outbreak, the Dalai Lama sent a letter to the general announcing his intention to meet with him—even though, as he confided to his readers, "I had no intention of going."[43]

---

40. Dalai Lama, *op. cit.*, p. 148.
41. *Ibid.,* p. 149.
42. *Ibid.,* p. 153.
43. *Ibid.*

Parenthetically, it is wonderful to read his praise of religions that "all teach us not to tell lies, or bear false witness, or steal, or take others' lives, and so on."[44] He reaffirms this conviction almost word for word in a more recent text that states, "All teach us not to lie or steal or take others' lives, and so on."[45]

Is Tibetan pacifism, whether atavistic or instilled in the people by an omnipotent religion, myth or reality? Let us allow the Dalai Lama himself to enlighten us:

"I do not pretend that every single Tibetan was a gentle and kindly person—of course we had our criminals and sinners. To mention a single example, we had many nomads, and though most of them were peaceful, some of their clans were not above brigandage. Consequently, settled people in certain neighborhoods had to take care to arm themselves, and travelers in such places preferred to go in large companies for protection. [. . . To the Khampas,] a rifle is almost more important than any other possession [. . .]."[46] At times, he says of his entire people, "I could not control their wish to resort to violence" or their "violent attitude."[47]

Furthermore, although he was adored by his happy people, "an escort of twenty-five armed guards accompanied the Dalai Lama wherever he went, and armed troops

---

44. *Ibid.*, p. 199.
45. Dalai Lama, "World Religions for World Peace," in *A Human Approach to World Peace*. Wisdom Publications, Boston, 1984.
46. Dalai Lama, The Dalai Lama, *My Land and My People, op. cit.*, p. 42.
47. *Ibid.*, p. 118 and 149 respectively.

were always posted along the route."[48] It is true that previous Dalai Lamas had been assassinated by hit men working on the orders of those closest to them.

About his army, he says, "Its main work was to man the frontier posts and to stop unauthorized foreigners (meaning, almost all foreigners) coming into the country. This army also formed our police force, except in the city of Lhasa, which had its own police, and in the monasteries" (p. 40). "[. . .] its strength was 8500 officers and men. There were more than enough rifles for them, but only about fifty pieces of artillery of various kinds—250 mortars and about 200 machine guns. [. . .] It was quite inadequate to fight a war."[49]

Observe that his reason is not a Gandhian love of non-violence, but the risk of defeat.

The Dalai Lama repeated this same analysis nearly half a century later, on May 12, 2008, in an interview with German magazine *Der Spiegel*. Once again, the religious leader's pacifism does not appear to be a natural outgrowth of his thoughts, but is instead imposed by the power dynamics at play: "[Would this mean] that the Tibetans should take up arms to achieve their independence? Which arms, and where would they come from? From the mujahedeen in Pakistan, perhaps? And if we get the weapons, how do we get them to Tibet? And once that armed war of inde-

---

48. *Ibid.*, p. 137.
49. *Ibid.*, p. 59.

pendence has begun, will the Americans come to our aid? Or the Germans?"

On April 29, 2005, His Holiness hinted to a group of French senators visiting his seat of exile in India that the Pentagon might be able to answer that last question. "America's policy is designed to promote democracy in Iraq and Afghanistan using sometimes controversial methods. I say so much the better, they are welcome. But it would be even better if they were to promote democracy in China."[50]

Does this make the Dalai Lama a defeated general pulling back to "previously prepared positions"? Does he practice the art of peace, or the art of war, with its offensives and withdrawals, truces and armistices, victories and defeats, propaganda and lies? Readers may make up their own minds once they have read what follows.

During his reign, the Dalai Lama's military inferiority and fear that Beijing would introduce sweeping reforms in Tibet pushed him to call on foreign powers, since "Tibet had neither the material resources nor the arms or men to defend its integrity against a serious attack." "Four delegations were appointed to visit Britain, the United States of America, India, and Nepal to ask for help."[51] Those countries flatly refused to support this warmongering and kept their soldiers at home. Washington even "declined to re-

---

50. Translation of the report by the Franco-Tibetan friendship group to the French Senate on June 14, 2006.
51. Dalai Lama, *My Land and My People, op. cit.*, p. 60.

ceive our delegation."[52] Now that "nobody would offer us any military help [. . .], we felt abandoned to the hordes of the Chinese army."[53]

The Dalai Lama tells of how he traveled to India to visit the tomb of Gandhi, "a true believer in peace and harmony among all men," and "wondered what wise counsel the Mahatma would have given me [. . .]."[54] Perhaps he might have suggested not asking for help from four foreign armies to invade a Chinese province, rain down death and destruction and keep it bound up in a theocratic straitjacket in which power—every power—is concentrated in the hands of a single man, the spiritual and temporal leader who cannot be challenged because he was produced by the divine miracle of an appropriate reincarnation.

And after all four foreign nations had refused the peaceable Dalai Lama's request for an armed intervention to preserve his power, then what happened? To hear him tell it, simply the "Tibetan people's peaceful uprising in Lhasa on 10 March 1959."[55]

"Peaceful," he called it. Beijing, on the contrary, claims that it was an armed insurrection. Who should we believe? Let us refer to the Dalai Lama's version of the events in his *Autobiography*.

"The Chinese announced at a public meeting [. . .]

---

52. *Ibid.*, p. 61.
53. *Ibid.*, p. 65.
54. *Ibid.*, p. 116.
55. Dalai Lama's Speech on the 49th Anniversary of the Tibetan National Uprising Day, in Dharamsala, March 10, 2008.

that revolt had broken out in the east against their rule, and that they were fully prepared to do whatever was needed to crush it.

This was a shock to the ministers [of the Dalai Lama]. They had known, of course, that the Khampas were fighting [. . .]."[56]

"The number of Khampas who had taken to the mountains as guerillas had grown from hundreds to tens of thousands. They had already fought some considerable battles [. . .]."[57]

"Tibetans could never be awed or terrified into acquiescence, and to attack our religion, our most precious possession, was a lunatic policy. The effect of these actions was simply to spread and intensify the revolt. [. . .] People were taking to arms throughout the east, northeast, and southeast of Tibet. It was only the western and central parts of the country which were still in comparative peace."[58]

"I was very unhappy too at this turn of events. It made my dilemma even more acute. Part of me greatly admired the guerilla fighters. They were brave people, men and women, and they were putting their lives and their children's lives at stake to try to save our religion and country in the only remaining way that they could see."[59]

The words seem to suggest that the entire population

---

56. *Ibid.*, p. 127.
57. *Ibid.*, p. 128.
58. *Ibid.*, p. 129.
59. *Ibid.*, p. 130.

rose up to fight in defense of the Dalai Lama and his entourage. Alexandra David-Néel's account is more qualified, asserting that the general population did not massively resist the arrival of the Chinese army. She also says that the peasants were not entirely unaware of the results achieved by agrarian reforms in China. "They looked forward to what might follow the Chinese troops."[60]

When the revolt against the central government in Beijing failed, despite being armed and urged along by the Dalai Lama behind the scenes, and the religious leader's troops were forced to fall back to India, he mustered up his manly pride and put on a uniform. On March 17, 1959, "around nine o'clock in the evening, I took off my Lama robes and put on a military uniform. [. . .] I took a rifle from one of [the soldiers] and slung it on my shoulder [. . .]."[61]

In the glowing portrait sketched by *Compassion: The Words and Inspiration of the Dalai Lama*[62], South-African journalist and author Mike Nicol presumes to point out, "Ironically, it was disguised as a soldier, with a rifle over his shoulder, that he stole out of Lhasa at night and headed for the Indian border with his retinue."[63] How bizarre that the rebel leader, a man who declared himself a pacifist when there was fighting to be done, should decide to put on a uniform and pick up a rifle to help him scurry for safety

---

60. Translation of David-Néel, Alexandra, *op. cit.*, p. 1016.
61. Dalai Lama, *My Land and My People, op. cit.*, p. 160.
62. *Compassion: The Words and Inspiration of the Dalai Lama*, preface by Desmond Tutu, introduction by Mike Nicol. Hachette Livre Australia, 2008.
63. *Ibid.*, p. 18.

more discreetly. Generally, if a defeated soldier is going to bolt, he disguises himself as a civilian—and besides, "peaceful" uprisings usually do without soldiers, since otherwise they are described by global consensus as "armed" instead.

David-Néel reports several details that the runaway and Nicol choose to omit, despite their crucial importance, having to do with the fate of the public treasury in this destitute region. "Many public officials went with him, as well as servants of different ranks, a caravan made up of more than a thousand mules and countless porters carrying crates full of gold and precious objects from the Potala Palace."[64]

---

64. Translation of David-Néel, Alexandra, *op. cit.*, p. 979-980.

4. An Appalling Regime:
Independence or Autonomy?

"The supremacy of the monastic orders in Tibet is something unique. It can well be compared to a stern dictatorship."[65]

Social advancement was easier for monks and members of the religious administration: "Some of them had large grants of land, and some had endowments [. . .]. Some acted as moneylenders, and a few charged rates of interest higher than I can approve."[66] Unfortunately, the book does not provide any figures, but interest varied between 20 and 50 percent. As if that was not enough, monks received subsidies from the government, "mainly of food [. . .]. These subsidies, of course, came ultimately from the rents or taxes of the laity."[67]

---

65. Harrer, Heinrich, Nazi officer and private tutor to the Dalai Lama. *Seven Years in Tibet.* Tarcher, New York, 1997.
66. Dalai Lama, *My Land and My People, op. cit.*, p. 40.
67. *Ibid.*

Depending on the circumstances, location, parties involved and what he perceives as his current interests, the Dalai Lama has at times asked for both autonomy within the China he loves, and complete independence from the China he despises. Ambiguity, contradictions and outright reversals are rampant. Does this reflect the understandable evolution of his thoughts over the years, or a two-faced approach from the start? And in the end, what does the Dalai Lama actually want? Independence? Or autonomy? The answer is given here by excerpts from his own speeches and writings, since the words of his detractors are, naturally, suspect.

Consider Corsica, a territorial collectivity of France. The difference between Corsica enjoying its special status as an island and Corsica campaigning for independence is that in the first instance, it would refer to mainland France as "the Continent," while in the second it would say simply "France," emphasizing that it is a foreign country. The same rule of thumb applies to everyone, everywhere.

It is particularly relevant to our current discussion of the Dalai Lama, who has virtually divided Tibet in half: the Tibetans on one side, and on the other the 55 other ethnic groups that make up China. He refers to these as "Chinese" and, occasionally, the "Chinese hordes".

Chapter 4 of his autobiography is entitled "Our Neighbor China," which clearly indicates that China is a foreign country, since "from 1912 until the fateful year of

1950, Tibet enjoyed complete de facto independence of any other nation."[68]

"Tibet has many neighbors: China, Mongolia, East Turkestan in the east and north, and India, Burma, and the states of Nepal, Sikkim, and Bhutan in the south. Pakistan, Afghanistan, and the Soviet Union are also close to us."[69]

At this point, readers might wonder why the Dalai Lama should want Tibet to become an autonomous region within one of these "foreign" countries, namely China.

Indeed, he makes barely any attempt to unravel the erratic tangle of ties between Tibet and China over the centuries. Never linear, these ties have sometimes been quite loose, such as when a European power (England) made the law with its army. As Alexandra David-Néel puts it, "Tibet's history has been intimately entwined with China's for centuries."[70]

The Dalai Lama seems to acknowledge this, saying, "I knew the Chinese would claim that Tibet had always been part of China" but going on to add, "In spite of our thirty-eight years of total freedom."[71]

This means that between the first Dalai Lama, Gend-un Drup, who passed away in 1474, and the 14th, Tenzin Gyatso, who ruled until 1959, nearly five centuries elapsed

---

68. Dalai Lama, *My Land and My People, The Original Autobiography of His Holiness the Dalai Lama of Tibet, op. cit.*, p. 57.

69. *Ibid.*, p. 37.

70. Translation of David-Néel, Alexandra, *op. cit.*, p. 964.

71. Dalai Lama, *My Land and My People, op. cit.*, p. 182.

during which Tibet experienced "thirty-eight years of total freedom." A short period of freedom indeed, and hardly total unless one ignores the British colonial presence.

Nonetheless, in the Dalai Lama's eyes, these fewer than forty years of relative independence seem to count for more than five centuries of shared life, whose continuation would dilute the uniqueness of the Tibetan race. This belief is described in the Five Point Peace Plan presented by the Dalai Lama to the U.S. Congressional Human Rights Caucus on September 21, 1987.

The address argued for strict racial purification in the "whole of Tibet," to be accomplished by the expedient of simply expelling all but the ethnic Tibetans. The Dalai Lama maintained that the 7.5 million intruders must leave the country as soon as he returns there himself, considering this "transfer" to be "imperative."

His plan also demands independence and differentiates between Tibetans, who are "different," and the 55 other Chinese ethnic groups who apparently represent a homogenous whole, even though most of them have their own culture, traditions and language. If the Dalai Lama were willing to accept that each ethnic group is unique, however, he would have to openly conclude and proclaim that China's natural destiny is to splinter into scores of tiny states.

Just imagine what would happen to France, a nation assembled from odds and ends, if independence were granted to the Basque country, Brittany and Provence, Corsica, the

Nice region and the overseas departments and territories. After all, Provence did not come under French rule until 1481, Brittany in 1532, Corsica in 1768 and the county of Nice in 1860. And what about France's far-off possessions that are wildly different from the mainland, like New Caledonia, a French archipelago located 17,000 km away from the rest of the country?

Since the idea of fragmentation was inconvenient for his personal claim, the Dalai Lama opted instead to describe China in terms of a dichotomy:

"There are open conflicts in the Middle East, Southeast Asia, and in my own country, Tibet."

"Under international law Tibet today is still an independent state under illegal occupation."

"Tibetans and Chinese are distinct peoples, each with their own country, history, culture, language, and way of life."

"It is China's illegal occupation of Tibet [. . .]"

"Tibet was a fully independent state when the People's Liberation Army invaded the country [. . .]"

"In 1982, [. . .] I sent my representatives to Peking to open talks concerning the future of my country and people."

"I hope this may contribute to a future of friendship and cooperation with all of our neighbours, including the Chinese people."[72]

---

72. Dalai Lama, address to the U.S. Congressional Human Right's Caucus on September 21, 1987.

On December 10, 1989, in his Nobel Prize acceptance speech, he informed the honorable assembly, "The suffering of our people during the past forty years of occupation is well documented."

It is easy to say that these speeches are dated, and the Dalai Lama has changed his tune. As I have explained, his plans are becoming frayed with time and repeated failure, although he still occasionally bursts forth with irrepressible calls for independence, his heart's dearest wish that he cannot quite prevent from slipping out. Because in fact, what he claims is not simply Tibet's historical autonomy (which it already has, as the Tibet Autonomous Region), but instead independence for what he calls "Greater Tibet," an immense territory that includes regions where ethnic Tibetans have always been the minority.

In a speech on "Buddhism and Democracy" given in Washington, D.C. in April 1993, consisting of generalized statements about democracy, the Dalai Lama asserted, "For many reasons, I have decided that I will not be the head of, or play any role in the government when Tibet becomes independent." On March 10, 2008, however, he gave a speech in Dharamsala, India in which he claims that Tibet's language, customs and traditions are gradually disappearing, and resumes his position as spokesman for the Tibetan people, saying, "I have a historical and moral responsibility to continue to speak out freely on their behalf." He also criticizes the organization of the autonomous regions as "autonomous in name only."

The French senators, however, saw the Autonomous Region of Tibet differently: "The TAR is home to just over two million of the six million Tibetans living in China.

The Law on Regional Ethnic Autonomy, adopted on May 31, 1984, defines a general framework for all of China's autonomous regions. Under this law, the People's Congress of the Tibet Autonomous Region has the power to enact local regulations enjoyed by an ordinary administrative region at the provincial level and the power to enact regulations on the exercise of autonomy as well as separate regulations in light of the political, economic and cultural characteristics of the ethnic group or ethnic groups in the region. The legislative body of the autonomous region may also modify or supplement certain state laws. For example, out of consideration for the special natural and geographical factors of Tibet, the Tibet Autonomous Region has fixed the work week at 35 hours, five hours fewer than the national statutory work week."[73]

But the most astonishing development was this: in March 2008, with the Beijing Olympic Games approaching, campaigns began to spring up abroad to push the Tibetan issue, outraging the Chinese population. It would have been a major mistake for the Dalai Lama not to distance himself from them. He did not wish to be associ-

73. Translation of the report by the interparliamentary friendship group of the French Senate on October 17, 2007; citing the white paper *Regional Ethnic Autonomy in Tibet*, Information Office of the State Council of the People's Republic of China. May 2004, Beijing.

ated with people who came across as enemies of China and destroyers of the Olympic dream, a dream the Tibetans share. The Olympic torch was scheduled to travel through the Tibetan capital of Lhasa and the Shannan region. On March 28, the Dalai Lama launched an "appeal to the Chinese people." Almost unbelievably, the text states, "Chinese brothers and sisters, I assure you I have no desire to seek Tibet's separation. Nor do I have any wish to drive a wedge between the Tibetan and Chinese peoples." He went on to "express these concerns both as a fellow human being and as someone who is prepared to consider himself a member of the large family that is the People's Republic of China," proclaiming his surprise at an unjust suspicion: "It is unfortunate that despite my sincere efforts not to separate Tibet from China, the leaders of the PRC continue to accuse me of being a 'separatist'."

Unimaginable! After all, the Dalai Lama has never hidden from the world his love for this "large family" of which he hopes to remain a member, made up of "ruthless" (p. 192) "invaders" (p. 73), who engaged in "pillaging," suffering as they did from "bad manners" (p. 74) that pushed them to commit "abominable" acts against Tibetans who "have not only been shot, but beaten to death, crucified, burned alive, drowned, vivisected, starved, strangled, hanged, scalded, buried alive, disemboweled, and beheaded" (p. 184). "Small children have even been forced to shoot their parents" (p. 184), and "many Tibetan men and women believe the Chinese have sterilized them" (p. 185).

In passing, let me point out that the members of an international commission convened by the Dalai Lama "examined every Chinese and Tibetan statement" (p. 183), but "did not accept their evidence as conclusive." This did not prevent the Dalai Lama from believing their accounts (p. 183) and propagating them, since after all the Chinese are "criminals" who used "methods reminiscent of the jungle" (p. 217), plunging Tibet into a "night of subjugation and oppression" (p. 222).[74]

One might object to the fact that I am comparing statements from 2008 with others from a book published in the 1960s. And it is true that in his March 2008 appeal, the Dalai Lama showed compassion to victims of every race, whether Han (he calls them "Chinese") or Tibetan:

"In the light of the recent developments in Tibet, I would like to share with you my thoughts concerning relations between the Tibetan and Chinese peoples, and make a personal appeal to all of you.

I am deeply saddened by the loss of life in the recent tragic events in Tibet. I am aware that some Chinese have also died. I feel for the victims and their families and pray for them. The recent unrest has clearly demonstrated the gravity of the situation in Tibet and the urgent need to seek a peaceful and mutually beneficial solution through dialogue."

Indeed, times have changed. The Dalai Lama's dream

---

74. Dalai Lama, *My Land and My People, op. cit.*

from a time when he believed he would be able to return to China (with help from the international community, which had first to be properly horrified) is no longer relevant since has realized that no armed intervention is possible (China now has nuclear weapons). Sufficiently effective economic or trade sanctions are equally out of the question. Despite their own qualms and reservations about the Chinese system, some of the intellectuals (authors, journalists, etc.) and politicians who have visited Tibet have lifted the veil from the former Tibet and observed that not all the changes have been negative.

And so the Dalai Lama is adapting to his circumstances; he has softened his language without ever explicitly retracting his previous statements. The one constant is a desire for independence, and he is tirelessly preparing for its arrival with his "government" in Dharamsala.

The publicity that erupted in the West around this business of exterminating the Tibetan population (through sterilization and massacres) created a deep well of compassion for Tibet and Buddhism. Nonetheless, it has been scientifically proven false by internationally recognized experts.[75]

The same goes for the figure of 1.2 million deaths caused by violence in Tibet since the 13th Dalai Lama fled. It was cooked up by the 14th Dalai Lama's "Tibetan gov-

75. Lucon, Gérard. "Tibet, une réalité démographique et des chiffres, des chiffres . . ." *Le Grand Soir.* September 17, 2010. http://www.legrandsoir.info/Tibet-une-realite-demographie-et-des-chiffres-des-chiffres.html.

ernment-in-exile," as international researchers have demonstrated.[76] Simply examining the population pyramid is
enough to put the lie to this tall tale, and even the Dalai
Lama no longer supports it. His accusation is no longer of
"genocide," but of "cultural genocide." Besides, how can
anyone talk about genocide against full-blooded Tibetans (the "pure race") when Tibet is exempt from the one-
child policy in effect across most Chinese regions, and the
("pure") population has grown spectacularly since 1959?

Such falsehoods leave room for doubt about the accu-

---

76. British writer Patrick French, a critical observer of Chinese policy and
former director of the Free Tibet Campaign, gained access to the archives of
the Dalai Lama's government in exile. He discovered that the evidence of genocide was false and resigned from his position. Specifically, he examined the
figures collected by one of the Dalai Lama's brothers, Gyalo Thondup. French
realized that, among other falsifications, the same person could be counted
as many as five times in the figures on those killed in confrontations with the
Chinese army, if five different refugees reported him. With these methods, the
death count out of Dharamsala (which was accepted and published worldwide)
reached 1.2 million, at a time when the male population of Tibet was 1.5 million. If this were true, Tibet's later population growth could be explained only
by polygamy and superhuman fertility rates. Élisabeth Martens also talked
about it in her book *Histoire du bouddhisme tibétain. La compassion des puis-
sants:* "Pocket calculator in hand, he tried to confirm the exorbitant figure of
'1.2 million victims.' Bitterly, French noted in his report, 'After just three days
of work, it became clear that the figure of 1.2 million Tibetan deaths could
not be accepted [. . .] Possibly the most disturbing thing was that the total
included only 23,364 women. That would have meant that 1,076,636 victims
were men, which is clearly impossible, since there were only about 1.25 million
male Tibetans in 1950 [. . .] It was disturbing, but I was forced to conclude
that even if the investigation [by the government in Dharamsala] was well in-
tentioned, it was statistically unusable and far from meeting Western standards
in my field. It was shocking!"

French, Patrick. *Tibet, Tibet. A Personal History of a Lost Land.* Harper
Perennial. London, 2004.

racy and authenticity of other accounts of violence. At the same time, only a complete innocent with no knowledge of history could possibly believe that a military power, in a land abandoned by its fleeing rebel leaders, would completely respect human rights or even international conventions. We know how our own armies have acted in various parts of the world—Madagascar, Indochina, Algeria and China, where they looted the Old Summer Palace—and even on our own soil, in Paris itself (French Muslims thrown into the Seine in October 1961, and the Charonne metro station massacre in February 1962). Sadly, others were probably similarly unscrupulous. The British, for example, subdued Tibet at gunpoint before pillaging, violating and destroying its monasteries.

If, as the French Senate reported in October 2007, Tibet remains a treasure of humanity and "the world's eye on Chinese development," it might be best for someone to remove the beam that has apparently been lodged in that eye without apparently bothering it.

The Dalai Lama, meanwhile, is wrong to silently ignore the crimes that his predecessors perpetrated for centuries, which were well established, often even crueler and offered the people no hope of an end in sight. No hope, because one does not depose an authority who was reborn for the sole purpose of ruling from a palace monastery in the capital.

On April 6, 2008, spurred on by the protests in Lhasa, the Dalai Lama reached out to "all Tibetans," stating, "We had already formulated our approach to seeking a solution to the Tibetan issue within the constitution of the PRC."

Note that by saying this, he admitted that the solutions he formerly sought would have been "outside its constitution," something we had long since realized.

On November 23, 2008, the New York Times home page was emblazoned with the words, "Dalai Lama warns exile leaders to be 'prudent'." Why?

The Dalai Lama had just addressed more than 500 delegates from around the world who had gathered for a week in Dharamsala, saying, "The next 20 years, if we are not careful, if we are not prudent in our plans, there is a great danger. It could lead to the danger of failure." In other words, things were not quite settled. "The delegates ended their weeklong conference Saturday saying that they had decided against seeking independence for now and that they would maintain the Dalai Lama's 'middle way' - his push for autonomy through measured compromise that falls short of calling for independence."[77]

This sounds suspiciously like the fox in the fable who, unable to reach the dangling grapes, remarks, "Oh, you aren't even ripe yet! I don't need any sour grapes."

But what exactly is this "middle way," a proposal presented by the Dalai Lama as innovative, conciliatory and acceptable to the powers governing China? In his speech to the European Parliament in Strasbourg on October 24,

---

77. "Dalai Lama warns exile leaders to be 'prudent'." NYTimes.com. November 23, 2008. http://www.nytimes.com/2008/11/23/world/asia/23iht-tibet.1.18066173.html

2001, he explained that the new proposal is to replace the "17-Point Agreement" that was "forced" on him by the central government in 1951. He described that agreement as only "autonomy on paper," even though it bound the government in Beijing "not to alter the existing political system in Tibet; not to alter the status, functions, and powers of the Dalai Lama; to respect the religious beliefs, customs and habits of the Tibetan people and protect the monasteries; to develop agriculture and improve the people's standard of living; and not to compel the people to accept reforms."[78] Not a bad deal—and yet this agreement was what pushed the nobles and Buddhists to foment the revolt that ended in their exile.

In his proposal on October 24, 2001, known as the "Strasbourg proposal," the Dalai Lama asked for Tibet to "enjoy genuine autonomy within the framework of the People's Republic of China. However, not the autonomy on paper imposed on us 50 years ago in the 17-Point Agreement, but a true self-governing, genuinely autonomous Tibet, with Tibetans fully responsible for their own domestic affairs, including the education of their children, religious matters, cultural affairs, the care of their delicate and precious environment, and the local economy. Beijing would continue to be responsible for the conduct of foreign and defense affairs."

Argumentative types may well ask: if that is autonomy,

---

78. Dalai Lama, *My Land and My People, op. cit.*, p. 68.

how exactly would he define independence?

It is as though the Dalai Lama wanted to parody *The Marriage of Figaro*: "So long as you make no attempt to influence our economy, laws, social customs, culture, education, religion, justice, environment, and anything else that might conflict with the decisions I make by virtue of my divine power, you may co-manage Tibet with me, especially if you stay outside it to protect my borders and commercial interests under the watchful and critical eye of the community of nations."

What a fiendishly clever approach that was, pretending to offer an equal partnership, a "middle way" in which both parties apparently enjoy equivalent prerogatives. By charting what appears to be a course halfway between independence and annexation, a shrewd negotiator could reverse that so-called equivalence, with Lhasa making only certain concessions to Beijing, and allowing it to keep the rest. A man's home is his castle, after all—but this particular man in his saffron robe has claimed the entire region as his home, and perhaps a few other surrounding regions as well.

Is it so hard to imagine why Beijing might consider this proposal a ruse and a rejection, and refuse even to receive a delegation to discuss the matter? Perhaps it is because that delegation would be representing a government led by the Dalai Lama, who keeps promising that he has "no desire to seek Tibet's separation," since he considers himself "a member of the large family that is the People's Republic of

China." Faced with such contradictions, the Chinese government has pushed for greater clarity by asking the Dalai Lama to accept one essential condition before any meeting: he must dissolve his "government," since China would otherwise be forced to recognize him as a foreign head of state making an official visit.

It should be no surprise that, when the Dalai Lama demands to be fully entrusted with the Tibetan culture, the voice of Victor Hugo echoes once again in our ears, railing against the smoke and mirrors that have blocked progress there and thinking:

"Ah, we know you! we know the clerical party. It is an old party. This it is which mounts guard at the door of orthodoxy. This it is, which has found for the truth those two marvellous supporters, ignorance and error! This it is, which forbids to science and to genius, the going beyond the missal, and which wishes to cloister thought in dogmas. Every step which the intelligence of Europe has taken, has been in spite of it. Its history is written in the history of human progress, but it is written on the back of the leaf. It is opposed to it all.

This it is, which caused Prinelli to be scourged for having said that the stars would not fall. This it is, which put Campanella seven times to torture for having affirmed that the number of worlds was infinite, and for having caught a glimpse at the secret of creation. This it is, which persecuted Harvey for having proved the circulation of the blood. In the name of Jesus, it shut up Galileo. In the name of Saint Paul, it imprisoned Christopher Columbus. To discover a law of the heavens was an impiety. To find a world was a heresy. This it is which anathematized Pascal in the name of religion, Montaigne in the name of morality, Molière in the name of both morality and of religion. Oh! yes, certainly, whoever you may be, who call yourselves the Catholic party and who are the clerical party, we know you. For a long time already the human conscience has revolted against you, and now demands of you, 'What is it that you wish of me?' For a long time already you have tried to put a gag on the human intellect.

You wish to be the masters of education."[79]

Although Hugo gave that speech a century and a half ago, his finger seems to be hovering even now over Lhasa and Dharamsala, ready to brush away a row of 14 Dalai Lamas.

Could anything demonstrate more clearly than these examples, taken not from the central government in Beijing but from the mouth or pen of the Dalai Lama himself, that he has not for one second stopped striving toward independence and a theocratic Tibet under his rule? Only his style of directing the fight has adapted to the changing times.

"Our inequality in the distribution of wealth was certainly not in accordance with Buddhist teaching, and in the few years when I held effective power in Tibet, I managed to make some fundamental reforms."[80]

---

79. Hugo, Victor, quoted in "Report upon public schools and education, in the state of Rhode Island," *op. cit.*, pp. 73-74.

80. *Ibid.*, p. 43.

Of course, those "few years" were actually nine, and even though he was relatively (too) young, the Dalai Lama relied on a regent and advisors and seemed mature enough to make some decisions himself (such as the decision to expand his massive home), a fact that he boasts about to underscore his early wisdom. As for "some fundamental reforms," it would have been helpful for the Dalai Lama to cite them and mention whether the measures were successful.

He did specify, however, that he appointed a committee of fifty members and that the "simplest reform was in the collection of taxes." Apparently, in addition to government taxes, "the district authorities could collect as much extra as they liked [. . .]. As this was permitted by law, the people had to pay up."[81] And what types of taxes were permitted? The list quickly approaches the ludicrous: there were taxes on weddings, births and deaths, planting trees in front of their hovels, animals, religious festivals, singing, dancing, drumming, ringing bells, crossing through a village, being sent to prison, being released from prison, unemployment, etc.

"The people had to pay up," and they did so voluntarily, knowing that it would cost much more to disobey. Lhasa replaced the profits from this legally sanctioned theft with a salary paid to tax collectors (still in money collected from the people).

---

81. *Ibid.*

Since the land that the serfs worked to exhaustion was state-owned, they had to pay rent, often by giving up part of their meager harvest to become "the main source of the government's stocks which were distributed to the monasteries, the army, and officials." Others paid in hours of labor (corvée) or else were "required to provide free transport for government officials, and in some cases for the monasteries too."[82] This meant serfs and slaves carrying burdens on their backs, which released the fragile monks, soldiers and government officials from the task. They used their own backs always and everywhere, since the wheel (an invention that dates back to 3500 B.C.) was forbidden. It was impossible even to consider allowing wheelbarrows (which the rest of China had been using since 100 B.C.) or carts pulled by beasts of burden, since those would "leave scars on the sacred surface of the earth." Not only did men exhaust themselves and die from the heavy burdens, but trade was hampered, living standards stagnated and the only road in Tibet was a single strip built on the Potala's Red Mountain in Lhasa so that the 13th Dalai Lama could drive up and down it in his three automobiles—which presumably possessed the divine power of not leaving any marks whatsoever. Nonetheless, bicycles and scooters appeared within his lifetime. In 1943, the regent to the 14th Dalai Lama (who was eight years old at the time) once again forbade their use, for the same reason mentioned above, which the

82. *Ibid.*, p. 43.

monks took it upon themselves to reinforce. Even lines of communication were off-limits; when the British occupiers attempted to build them, they were told that the heavens would be offended and punish the neighborhood.[83]

Since "the right to demand transport had been given to far too many people" and corvée labor had only expanded with each successive Dalai Lama, the 14th decided, in a fit of compassionate and yet carefully limited democratic zeal, not to abolish the abomination but to increase the fees due for transportation that was not part of an obligatory corvée, determined for each case by a "special sanction."[84]

Still, "the most urgent single reform" had to do with the powers of the landlords who, like the monks in their monasteries, "exercised a feudal right of justice." And alas, just as the Dalai Lama was preparing to act on the reports from his reform committee, as he says, and dispossess estate owners who had received their land on loan, which would now be "distributed among the peasants who already worked it"[85], just as he was contemplating a second step of taking away the monasteries' land as well, the "Chinese invaders" put down the revolt that he was secretly directing, seized the power left vacant by his flight and deprived him of the pleasure of eliminating the "faults of [Tibet's]

---

83. Candler, Edmund. *The Unveiling of Lhasa*. New Delhi. Pentagon Press, 1987. Republished in 2007.
84. Dalai Lama, *My Land and My People, op. cit,* p. 43.
85. *Ibid.,* p. 45.

system." The Dalai Lama neatly summarizes the situation as follows: "More drastic events overtook us, and for the present it had to be abandoned."[86]

Though stymied in his task, the Dalai Lama was happy to note the work he had already accomplished: "So we had made a beginning in changing our social system from the medieval to the modern [. . .]."[87]

But what exactly did that medieval social system entail? The current Dalai Lama evades the question, and it is easy to see why. Thirteen Dalai Lamas before him, and he himself for nine years, accepted and even profited from a genocidal, mind-destroying, brutal system; even if his predecessor did make some infinitesimal reforms, and the 14th Dalai Lama succeeded in filing down a few of its sharper corners, the system itself remained an insult to democracy. We may well wonder which parts of it he condemns and which parts he considers so much gentler than the system established after his flight, which he continually denounces to the world as a living hell where there was once heaven on earth ("so we were happy").

Was the old system genocidal? Yes—the backward theocracy was so ruthless that during its reign, the population had stagnated at just over one million inhabitants for two centuries. Given the short lives of the serfs and the pious abstinence of a quarter of the male population, the Tibetan people risked extinction in the event of an epidemic or a

86. *Ibid.*, p. 46.
87. *Ibid.*

75

food shortage. When the British came to Tibet with formally educated physicians, bearing the modern, scientific knowledge that was used everywhere else in the world to ease pain, heal disease and slow the march toward death, they were met with hostility from the monks. The so-called ethnic genocide that the Tibetan people are supposed to have suffered at the hands of the central Beijing government lurked palpably around the edges of poverty-stricken villages where years, decades and centuries passed without in any way alleviating the suffering of the penniless families who clung to life there.

Was it mind-destroying? Yes. Education, which is known to spread atheism and secularism, was withheld from the common people, while the Buddhist elite spent interminable years studying. The main product of this learning was an incomprehensible jargon that awed the serfs and persuaded them of their inferiority, grooming them for a life of humility and obedience. Mind-destroying also, because Buddhist texts replaced all other knowledge not only among the common people, but also for the vast majority of the country's lords and masters, who were never taught science. Once again, when the British occupiers tried to open schools, the monks made their disapproval clear.

It was mind-destroying in yet another way: the serfs could not travel, even to Lhasa, and never once in their lives met a foreigner with a different culture and different knowledge. Finally, the poor wretches were so exhausted by their labor that they no longer had the time or strength to think for themselves. Seen in this light, the Dalai Lama begins to seem like the head of a religion or philosophy that has been debased almost to the point of a sect, reigning over a million captive followers within closed borders, hidden away from the eyes of the world. *Cult*

The word "sect" may seem harsh—but what is a sect? In short, an extremist and uncompromising religious organization whose leaders deny their disciples every individual freedom, force them to perform rituals and mentally manipulate them to keep them under control. The organization is a pyramid scheme, with power concentrated in the hands of one charismatic authority: a guru. Kept in ignorance of other doctrines or practices, the followers are subjected to living conditions that keep them exhausted (lack of rest and food, endless tasks), inhibiting their intellectual abilities. The sect lines its own pockets with their money and possessions, leaving its followers completely dependent.

So I will leave it up to each reader to decide, was it a sect, or not? (The Info-Sectes association is following events closely, but has not yet taken a side.) Either way, brutality and devastation were the norm, and they generated incredible wealth for the corrupt:

"Drepung monastery was one of the biggest landowners in the world, with its 185 manors, 25,000 serfs, 300 great pastures, and 16,000 herdsmen. The wealth of the monasteries went to the higher-ranking lamas, many of them scions of aristocratic families [. . .]. Along with the upper clergy, secular leaders did well. A notable example was the commander-in-chief of the Tibetan army, who owned 4,000 square kilometers of land and 3,500 serfs. He also was a member of the Dalai Lama's lay Cabinet."[88]

The serfs belonged to their lord, who could punish or sell them. They were not allowed to leave his land. They had to seek his permission to marry. They could even be demoted to the rank of slaves. If they were unmanageable, they were punished with wooden cages, shackles on their feet, iron collars, slit tongues, hands or feet, and gouged eyes (with boiling water to heal the open wounds), or put to death by being tied up in a leather sack and thrown into the river. To escape this justice, they had to toe the line, pay countless taxes (see above), perform corvée labor for up to 80 percent of their working hours and supply their masters with quintals of grain. They were so destitute that they had to borrow money from the monks, nobles and landowners in order to pay for the food they had produced and handed over to those castes according to the law. Usurious interest rates made them debtors for life, and their debts could even accumulate across generations into a sort of negative inheritance, which many peasants had. The Preparatory Committee for the Tibet Autonomous Region, a working entity created by Beijing and chaired by the Dalai Lama, cancelled these debts on July 17, 1959, a few months after he fled into exile.

---

88. Stuart and Roma Gelder, *The Timely Rain*, *op. cit.*, p. 62 and 174.

Since no new agricultural knowledge was allowed into Tibet, no modern tools or techniques were available to tame the harsh climate and dry soil. Crop yields were disastrous. Cattle and sheep died too quickly to breed a herd, and typhoid ran fatally rampant.

Between 1927 and 1952, more than 90 percent of the families in certain villages chose to brave retaliation, escape and seek their happiness outside Tibet. "And so we were happy," says the Dalai Lama, and "I had started to make reforms."

It is fair to say that although his predecessor, the 13th Dalai Lama, did not go so far as to end serfdom and slavery, he did outlaw several of the cruelest abuses, even abolishing the death penalty in 1898 (it was 1981 in France)—at least on paper, since there were executions after that date. In 1923, he founded the first English school in Gyantse, the third-largest city in the country. It was forced to close barely three years later, however, by the opposition of monks whipped into a frenzy by their long training in intentionally blocking progress and rejecting foreigners.

The official translation of the *Guidelines for Future Tibet's Polity and Basic Features of Its Constitution*, published by the Dalai Lama on February 26, 1992, tells us, "Tibet has a recorded history of over 2,000 years, and according to archaeological findings, a civilization dating back to over 4,000 years." If this is true, how is it possible that in the first half of the 20th century, the region was still so ignorant of the discoveries that had spread throughout the rest of the world over the years? Is it because of Tibet's unique geographical situation? Partly, no doubt. And yet the oceans and seas are littered with other places that are equally (if not more) isolated, and yet progress has reached them. In Tibet, there was a deliberate desire to petrify society and freeze its politics and religion in a configuration that benefited a minority, which was loath to give up what it had experienced as a happy and prosperous Middle Age. This minority feared that lifting the blindfold of ignorance even the slightest bit would reveal that in France, Europe and many other lands, the Enlightenment had planted new ideas about the government of human societies, transforming the lives of the poor as they developed.

The scholars, philosophers and writers who helped generate these ideas taught their students to criticize absolutism, claimed that private interests should be set aside in favor of the general interest and insisted on promoting economic progress and secular humanism, spreading education everywhere, making technical knowledge widely accessible and tearing down prejudice of all kinds. These heretics contended that talent should prevail over birth privilege. They claimed to be able to give meaning to the world and transform it with intellectual tools. They insisted that reason could and should challenge any customs, traditions and laws that impeded justice.

This plague was not to be allowed to pollute Tibet. Nonetheless, with the passing years, the Dalai Lama's regent and advisers and the aristocrats began to realize that, to secure their own comfort, they would need a few educated Tibetans who understood English to run their equipment, such as a hydroelectric plant and radio transmitters. The marvelous region was so technologically backward that there was not a single citizen capable of stepping up to the task. Consequently (or out of desperation), a modest school was opened in Lhasa, in mid-summer 1944, where classes were taught in Tibetan and English.

But alas! No matter how often the regent explained that the new school was simply an extension of the 13th Dalai Lama's policies, the monks were so hysterically indignant that it had to close its doors six months later.

We have not read anything from the Dalai Lama to suggest that he took any concrete steps to rectify the situation. The illiteracy of his "happy" people apparently did not worry him, and the few reforms he boasts of having accomplished did not include opening schools in Tibet.

Some may reproach me for failing to compare the Dalai Lama's ideas in 1959 with those he professed a half-century later, when he had reached the age of wisdom. Unfortunately, such a comparison will not reassure those who favor free, compulsory, secular schools and the development of scientific knowledge. When traveling abroad and addressing audiences other than his own illiterate followers, who have been indoctrinated by more than a 100,000 monks churned out by 2,700 monasteries, the Dalai Lama naturally cannot sing the praises of the widespread ignorance that made his ruling class rich, and so he does speak of education. Yet although he manages not to rehash old prejudices dazzlingly clothed in the absolute supremacy of spiritual over material concerns, he never seems overly enthusiastic about the miracles that education can accomplish, nor does he fail to denounce its more pernicious effects. He does this with a carefully measured, balanced approach: one dose of approval for education, which does provide lowly material comfort, mixed with one dose of regret for the blessed time when, living in the meadows of ignorance (read: thanks to that ignorance), people developed the mental virtues they needed to be happy.

In his Nobel Prize lecture on December 10, 1989, in a place where the very highest honor is awarded to brilliant minds in various scientific fields, the Dalai Lama said, "Material progress is of course important for human advancement. In Tibet, we paid much too little attention to technological and economic development, and today we realize that this was a mistake." Having brushed aside what he modestly calls "a mistake" (the intentionally deficient educational system), which he seems to suggest occurred in only two fields (in fact, they all suffered), the Dalai Lama waxes eloquent about love, kindness, inner happiness, calmness, tranquility and deep peace, all of which are at risk from a threat that he clearly identifies: "At the same time, material development without spiritual development can also cause serious problems. [. . .] I believe both are important and must be developed side by side so as to achieve a good balance between them." The underlying message of the succeeding paragraphs is that by definition, the knowledge which generates technological progress has no conscience, and leads to "ruin for the soul." Does he realize that history is filled with examples of entire peoples who, after reading books and listening to their most learned members, threw themselves into altruistic efforts for peace, justice, love of the most vulnerable, solidarity and the right to happiness for all (not just a single caste)?

In the *Guidelines* cited above, the Dalai Lama mournfully states, "Although technological advancement has brought material prosperity to much of today's world, it has also resulted in the loss of respect for human beings."

Anyone can see that the Dalai Lama is not questioning an economic system that creates harsher relationships between individuals and entire peoples; technology is the real enemy. To believe this, we must forget that during the era when the Dalai Lamas sheltered their people from any type of progress, innovation or education, Tibet "had many nomads, and [. . .] some of their clans were not above brigandage. Consequently, settled people in certain neighborhoods had to take care to arm themselves."[89] In his *Guidelines*, the Dalai Lama goes on to say, "Human beings have also lost much of their freedom, so much so that they have become the slaves of machines."[90]

One could almost believe that the wheel was what en-

---

89. Dalai Lama, *My Land and My People, op. cit.*, p. 42.
90. Dalai Lama, *Guidelines for Future Tibet's Polity and Basic Features of Its Constitution*, February 26, 1992.

slaved these Tibetans, who were once free porters in the "happiest of lands." One could almost forget that it is not some insane love or unreasonable passion that ties men to their machines, but rather the laws of labor and profit, which the Dalai Lama never vilifies. Neither do we ever hear him call for less work and more free time, except no doubt for the monks, who are exempt from any productive activity and free of any commitments that could keep them from their meditation.

Let us return to another of his texts, *A Human Approach to World Peace*. After having solemnly affirmed (and why should he even feel the need to do so?), "I am not at all against science and technology," the Dalai Lama lingers repeatedly over their disadvantages. Through them, "We are in danger of losing touch with those aspects of human knowledge and understanding that aspire towards honesty and altruism." "Science and technology, though capable of creating immeasurable material comfort, cannot replace the age-old spiritual and humanitarian values [. . .]." Certainly not, and there are no doubt millions of us who, without the guidance of advertising agencies, would be able to say the same thing. But he adds, "There is unprecedented literacy, yet this universal education does not seem to have fostered goodness, but only mental restlessness and discontent instead."

In his *Story of a Good Brahmin*, a fable that could have been written for the Dalai Lama, Voltaire tells of the meeting between a traveler and a Hindu priest, who lives next door to an old woman. She "believed with all her heart in the changing forms of the Lord Vishnu, and, provided she could occasionally have some water from the Ganges to wash in, she considered herself the happiest of all women." The Brahmin admits, "I have told myself a hundred times that I would be happy if I were as stupid as my neighbor, and yet I would want no part of that kind of happiness." The author then states his famous aphorism, "I would not want to be happy on condition of being ignorant," and concludes, "I found no one who wanted to accept the bargain of becoming ignorant in order to become content."

In this area, may we prefer Voltaire's wisdom from 1761 to the Dalai Lama's, and modern Tibet to the old Tibet?

5. NGOs and the CIA[91]

There is no need to be a conspiracy theorist to see the CIA lurking behind a gossamer web of front companies.

In 1960s France, the Congress for Cultural Freedom was an international movement of "free and independent" intellectuals who joined forces to fight Stalinism; they also published two magazines. Raymond Aron, the friend and intellectual opponent of Jean-Paul Sartre, was one of its most brilliant and best-known leaders. In his Memoirs[92], he tells of his embarrassment upon discovering that the association was partially financed by American funds provided indirectly by the CIA.

Another arm of the CIA is known as the NED (National Endowment for Democracy). In the 1980s, the endowment financed an extreme right-wing student organization called UNI, and today, it is one of the CIA front

---

91. Some of the information on this topic is taken from my book: Vivas, Maxime, *La Face cachée de Reporters sans frontières. De la CIA aux faucons du Pentagone.* Paris, Aden, 2007.

92. Aron, Raymond. *Memoirs: Fifty Years of Political Reflection.* Holmes and Meier, 1990.

agencies that subsidizes Reporters Without Borders (RWB, also know as Reporters Sans Frontières, or RSF), a French NGO that spearheaded the anti-China offensive to disrupt the Olympic torch relay in Paris in April 2008.[93] The Dalai Lama has also been supported for decades by the CIA and the NED, which in turn sponsors scores of organizations tasked with using Tibet to undermine China.

But what is the NED?

The American intelligence and subversion factory cannot directly underwrite organizations or programs that must appear to be free and national, or they risk being discredited. Whenever possible, therefore, it must work through go-betweens like the NED—not a private entity, but a government agency. Its money comes from the Department of State, which like the CIA is a department of the executive branch responsible for foreign policy. Republican and Democratic members of Congress are in agreement about the CIA's activities. The administration decides, the senators (from both sides) vote, and companies serving as screens collect and redistribute the cash: "The National Endowment for Democracy [was] created 15 years ago to do in the open what the Central Intelligence Agency has done surreptitiously for decades."[94]

In 1986, NED president Carl Gershman admitted, "It

---

93. See subsequent chapters.
94. Broder, John M., "Political Meddling by Outsiders: Not New for U.S.," *New York Times*, March 31, 1997.

would be terrible for democratic groups around the world to be seen as subsidized by the CIA. [. . .] We have not had the capability of doing this, and that's why the endowment [the NED] was created."[95] And on September 22, 1991, Allen Weinstein, who helped draft the legislation establishing the NED in 1983, acknowledged to the *Washington Post*, "A lot of what we do today was done covertly 25 years ago by the CIA."

In Nicaragua, to sway the February 1990 elections in which the Sandinista party was defeated, the CIA and NED set up a so-called civic society as a front (Via Civica). In Venezuela, the NED's budget quadrupled in the months leading up to the April 2002 coup against President Hugo Chavez. After the Soviet collapse, the NED was active in many Eastern countries that offered fertile ground for governments hostile to Russia and favorable to NATO.

At some point in their career, most key CIA figures have been associated with the NED, either as board members or other officials. One such man is John Negroponte, who was later appointed ambassador to occupied Iraq and, upon his return to the United States, became the country's first Director of National Intelligence (in this role, he was responsible for appointing the director of the CIA).

The NED website[96] has three additional categories for China in the "Where We Work" section: China (Hong Kong), China (Tibet) and China (Xinjiang).

---

95. *New York Times*, June 1, 1986.
96. http://www.ned.org

Even setting aside its secret operations (since, by definition, we know nothing about them), the CIA is involved in
Tibet, via the NED, through no fewer than 16 multi-facet-
ed programs that it openly subsidizes[97]: Bodkyi Translation
and Research House ($15,000), Consultations Samdup
($50,000), Gu-Chu-Sum Movement of Tibet ($43,675),
International Campaign for Tibet, or ICT ($50,000), Inter-
national Tibet Support Network ($45,000), Khawa Karpo
Tibet Culture Centre ($25,000), Students for a Free Tibet
($22,506), Tibet Museum ($15,000), Tibetan Centre for
Human Rights and Democracy, or TCHRD ($50,000),
Tibetan Institute for Performing Arts, or TIPA ($15,000),
Tibetan Literacy Society ($35,000), Tibetan Parliamentary
and Policy Research Centre, or TPPRC ($15,000), Tibetan
Review Trust Society ($25,000), Tibetan Women's Associa-
tion, Central ($15,000), Voice of Tibet ($33,600) and Wel-
fare Society Tibetan Chamber of Commerce ($15,000).

Those are just the tip of the iceberg.

Do not let the names of these programs and organizations fool you. On many occasions, American propaganda
has demonstrated its ability to speak ironically, referring to
the bloodiest dictatorships as "democracies" and champion-
ing freedom while opening more and more prisons around
the world, from Bagram (Afghanistan) to Abu Ghraib (Iraq)
to Guantanamo Bay (Cuba)—not to mention the astound-
ing number of prisons within United States borders and its

---

97. http://www.ned.org, January 2011.

secret "floating prisons." According to a study by the International Centre for Prison Studies at King's College London, with 2.3 million criminals behind bars, the United States has an incarceration rate of 743 per 100,000 of national population, the highest in the world, before Russia and Belarus.[98]

But to get back to the cash: since his flight from China, the Dalai Lama has quietly been receiving subsidies from the CIA.

Between 1959 and 1972, he was personally paid 180,000 dollars each year, a fact he long denied. Whatever its other faults, however, the United States does have enviable laws requiring official documents to be declassified after a certain period of time, which varies depending on the type of document. In 1998, the documents spilled their secrets, and the Dalai Lama's "government" had to admit what had already been made public while carefully rebutting the claim that His Holiness had profited "personally" from the money—although the Dalai Lama's representative in Washington maintained that he was aware of neither the subsidy nor how it was spent. As to the ties between the CIA and the Dalai Lama, he did acknowledge, "It is an open secret. We do not deny it."[99]

The Dalai Lama also received 1.7 million dollars to carry out his international political activities; the same amount was later paid via the NED.

98. AFP, June 27, 2005.

99. Mann, Jim. "CIA Gave Aid to Tibetan Exiles in '60s, Files Show." *Los Angeles Times*, September 15, 1998.

In monthly newspaper *Le Monde diplomatique*, Martine Bulard wrote, "[. . .] The CIA's financing of the Tibetan organization is not just a fantasy dreamed up by Chinese communists: in the sixties, the American agency apparently handed over 1.7 million dollars, and the *New York Times* investigation ('Dalai Lama Group Says It Got Money from C.I.A.' October 2, 1998) mentions a—modest yet significant—annual subsidy of 180,000 dollars paid directly to the religious leader, who denied the reports."[100]

Reporters Without Borders has organized protests against China on the basis of a prejudice that appears permanently on its website. For example, the site lists the Asian countries officially recognized by the international organizations, and tacks on Tibet on its own initiative. This is RWB's way of formally granting the Chinese region an independence that the UN does not recognize and the Dalai Lama himself shrewdly claims no longer to want.

In 2008, was the aim of RWB to promote greater freedom in Tibet? If so, everyone would certainly agree with its objectives, if not necessarily its methods. Was it defending the Tibetan media? Actually, examining the organization's activities and statements shows that RWB is engaged in a long-standing international political effort to separate Tibet from China.

In 2001, members of the NGO joined forces with activists from France-Tibet, an organization advocating for

---

100. Translation of Bulard, Martine, "Défendre le Tibet sans (forcément) encenser le dalaï-lama." *Le Monde diplomatique*, August 2008.

Tibetan independence, to heckle Chinese president Hu Jintao as he was leaving the French Institute for International Relations (Ifri). According to France-Tibet's website on November 5, 2001, "Our group included six members of Reporters Without Borders, including secretary-general Robert Ménard, and three France-Tibet activists. [. . .] Brandishing Tibetan flags while everyone chanted, 'Democracy in China! Freedom for Tibet!' our friends from RWB threw leaflets at the delegation calling for the release of Tibetan Ngawang Choephel and other political prisoners."

For many years, RWB has taken a much more pointed approach than the other NGOs who are actually responsible for monitoring these specific issues, such as Amnesty International. In fact, on March 25, 2008, the Amnesty France coordinator for China declared that her organization was "against any boycotts, including of the (Olympic) opening ceremonies, by politicians."

Although the Dalai Lama said the same thing, the RWB attacked, driven by a sacred mission that delighted its sponsors across the Atlantic.

On April 3, 2008, Tibet-Info proclaimed, "Whenever the torch passes through a city, we will be there to say, 'Don't forget the reality of Tibet, don't forget the reality of China,' said Ménard." Again, China and Tibet are described as two countries.

On April 6, 2008, the RWB website read, "Reporters Without Borders is calling all Parisians to assemble at the base of the Eiffel Tower starting at noon, wearing t-shirts depicting the Olympic rings as handcuffs or dressed in black, to demonstrate for human rights in China and in Tibet."

In China AND in Tibet! The appeal clearly states that there are two distinct countries and proves that an organization whose stated purpose is to defend journalists is now crusading in general for "human rights," and in particular to redefine the borders of an Asian country, both roles usually assigned to other entities.

Former U.S. President George W. Bush, for example, is an expert on human rights, as he demonstrated in Afghanistan and Iraq. That may be why, on April 8, 2008, RWB wrote him a courteous letter asking him not to attend the Olympic Games Opening Ceremony in Beijing. After that, even in his book published in October 2008, Robert Ménard avoided any further scrutiny of the American president.

On June 25, 2008, RWB urged the International Olympic Committee to demand an apology from China for statements made in Lhasa by Chinese officials, one of whom was quoted as saying, "We should firmly smash the plots to ruin the Beijing Olympic Games by the Dalai clique and hostile foreign forces."[101] Once again, Ménard was on extremely slippery ground here, forgetting his primary mission and acting as an ambassador responsible for defending the Dalai Lama in Europe.

---

101. Speech by Zhang Qingli in Lhasa, in front of the Potala Palace, on June 21, 2008. Reported by AFP on June 26, 2008.

The opening ceremony went forward smoothly for the organizers and international athletes (except the French team), awing the world with its splendor. RWB watched the proceedings bitterly. Although the Chinese people had experienced a complete change of heart about France, the Chinese authorities kept their heads. Perhaps it was time for RWB to goad the French government further? Here is what Ménard wrote at the time: "Nicolas Sarkozy was in the stands on August 8 in Beijing, seated alongside a row of great democratic figures: the presidents of Vietnam, Pakistan and Russia. . . and George Bush as well."[102] Ménard mentioned Bush only at the end, apparently reluctantly, like a required penance; neither he nor RWB had anything to add on that score. Others were not so lucky, and Reuters titled a wire story on August 4, 2008, "Robert Ménard is very angry:"

"By handling China with kid gloves, Nicolas Sarkozy is participating in a 'coalition of cowards' that includes the president of the International Olympic Committee (IOC), Jacques Rogge,' declared the secretary-general of Reporters Without Borders."

Note that this "coalition of cowards" includes the French president (for whom Ménard claims to have voted in the presidential elections), but not the then-resident of the White House, the executioner of Iraq (where more than 200 journalists and similar professionals died) and Afghanistan and supervisor of the Guantanamo torturers.

---

102. Translated from Ménard, Robert, *op. cit.*, p. 20.

In his book, the activist complains, "If you type 'Robert Ménard + CIA' into Google, the search engine generates . . . 114,000 hits."[103] Although the number was lower when I checked, it is still very high.

Let's see why.

I have already mentioned that the National Endowment for Democracy (NED) subsidizes the Dalai Lama; it also supports Reporters Without Borders, which has even received funding from the Taiwan Foundation for Democracy. On January 28, 2007, while he was secretary-general of RWB, Robert Ménard visited Taiwan to receive a check for 100,000 dollars from President Chen Shui-bian himself, on behalf of this foundation whose activities are directed at China.

When I wrote my book about RWB[104], I asked Robert Ménard to send me a copy of the contract between his organization and the NED. I never received it. I was able, however, to read a document on a United States government website in which the NED explains the commitments that its NGO beneficiaries must accept. NGOs must state specific objectives they are trying to reach in the country where their project is based. An example might be developing leadership skills among activists or improving the organizational abilities of local associations. They must provide concrete proof of the changes or results they have achieved: electoral results, laws enacted, court minutes, legislative or

---

103. *Ibid.*, p. 127.
104. Vivas, Maxime, *op. cit.*

legal documents, media coverage, etc. These obligations explain the RWB policy toward certain countries.

The NED goes on to say, however, that funded NGOs must not be involved in any activities designed to influence United States public policy. This prohibition has made it nearly impossible for RWB to condemn or put an end to the murder of journalists in Yugoslavia, and later in Iraq and Afghanistan, when the American army was involved. Likewise, RWB could not condemn Bush's attendance at the Olympic Games opening ceremony, although it had no such compunction about other heads of state.

Finally, if we assume that the United States, anxious about the rise of a great power and eager to remain the master of a unipolar world, is financing the Dalai Lamist separatist movement as a means to weaken China or even gain a foothold (and military bases) on the "Roof of the World," then it is no surprise to see RWB working feverishly for that same goal.

On Friday, September 26, 2008, Robert Ménard astonished the world by announcing that he would be leaving RWB the following Tuesday because he "wanted to do something else." Apparently looking for that something else, he spun his wheels for a while, publicly considered several options and ultimately went to peddle his services in Qatar, a misogynistic, polygamist Arabic dictatorship, where foreign workers are treated like the serfs in Tibet under the Dalai Lamas (the UN's Special Rapporteur on trafficking in persons, especially in women and children, has expressed her concern about immigrant workers who are victims of "human trafficking" in a place where flogging is a legal punishment, the death penalty is practiced, the press is not allowed to criticize the royal family in power and the laws come not from representatives elected by the people, but from Sharia).

These days, Ménard pontificates on a private television channel where, according to an article in a major French weekly, he "scoffs at" human rights "every morning on his show, humiliating and insulting his guests."[105]

---

105. Translated from Besson, Patrick, "L'interview selon Robert Ménard." *Le Point*, November 25, 2010.

6. Fanatics and the Olympic Flame

"To use the language of the May 1968 revolution, we need to 'create havoc in Beijing.' That means that during the Olympics, we'll jump, run and swim, but at the same time we need citizen athletes who will wear orange scarves and armbands, the symbols of the Ukrainian revolution, to proclaim their solidarity with Tibet."[106]

Reporters Without Borders is headquartered in Paris and claims to be an NGO defending journalists and press freedom around the globe. Most of the journalists who founded it soon walked out in the aftermath of disagreements, leaving it in the hands of Robert Ménard; after an abortive career as a student of philosophy, he had languished in the honey industry and then door-to-door insurance sales before giving in to the temptation of the media.

---

106. Cohn-Bendit, Daniel, Member of the European Parliament.

According to the RWB website, "Reporters Without Borders is present in all five continents through its national branches (in Austria, Belgium, Canada, France, Germany, Italy, Spain, Sweden and Switzerland), its offices in London, New York and Washington, and the more than 140 correspondents it has in other countries," which rely on local associations in some 15 countries.

RWB enjoys palatial quarters in Paris. It has 23 employees on the payroll and a budget of nearly 3.8 billion euros, of which only 22,000 euros (less than 0.6%) are provided by member dues. For the rest, it rakes in various grants and subsidies from large French companies, the French government, the European Union and the United States, and it constantly appeals to the generosity of the people. One corporate contributor is Carrefour, a big box chain with stores sprouting up all over China. Without citing an actual figure, RWB indicates that it receives European Commission grants intended in part to support the work of anti-government Chinese bloggers.

The French public believes it is defending press freedom by buying planners, calendars, photo albums, badges, comics, bags, DVDs, t-shirts and so on from the RWB store. These supporters may not realize, however, that the year before the concerted effort to disrupt the Olympic torch relay in Paris, Robert Ménard was invited to China by the Chinese government. He was received there as a distinguished guest, and he was told and shown things that, while they were probably not sufficiently convincing to win this former anarchist, Trotskyist, socialist and Sarkozy-ist over to the side of the Chinese Communist Party, may at least have eroded his usual tendency to see things in black and white.

In a book released after the Olympic games, he claimed that during his brief stay in China, his hosts made a series of commitments: "Eventually, we agreed on some written terms. We would stop our campaign and they would free the dissidents—starting with Zhao Yan, a researcher for the *New York Times*. They would free their prisoners, relax their internet controls, establish new working rules for foreign correspondents and allow Reports Without Borders to visit prisons where journalists were being held, and also open an office in Beijing. It was a great deal."[107] In fact, it was a coup that had not been accomplished in several years of collective efforts by global diplomacy and by every international association with an interest in advancing democracy in China. Despite this, Ménard was disappointed on his return to Paris, saying, "The Chinese media have published our agreement without the commitments by the authorities!"[108]

In vain, I tried to obtain the text of that agreement. The Chinese Embassy in Paris denies its existence, and RWB was unable to provide me with a copy, instead offering a "press release" from January 23, 2007 that was writ-

---

107. Translated from Ménard, Robert. *Des libertés et autres chinoiseries.* Paris, Robert Laffont, 2008, p. 85.
108. *Ibid.*

ten in Paris, in no way resembles a bilateral agreement and does not mention the specific points that Ménard listed in his book. In the press release, RWB expresses its wish that "these games will be a success, an occasion for all participating countries to share in the humanistic values of the Olympic idea." It fails to mention its own six-year campaign to prevent the Games from being held in China.

Indeed, on June 13, 2001, French Dalai Lamist site Tibet-Info claimed that "to Ménard, holding the Olympics in Beijing was 'just as monstrous' as it had been to hold them in Nazi Germany in 1936." In other words, at the time, RWB was agitating not for a boycott of the Olympic Games opening ceremony, but rather for the Games not to be held in Beijing at all. The same site goes on to say that RWB had even sent "a press file to the 123 members of the IOC, entitled Au nom des droits de l'homme, non à la candidature de Pékin 2008," in an attempt to block Beijing's bid by painting the city as a "risky choice" because China "is a repressive and unstable country."

For reasons of its own, RWB went even further than the Dalai Lama, who never publicly called for a boycott of either the Games or the opening ceremony.

In Paris and elsewhere, Robert Ménard set off a frenzied round of activism, pouring all the resources of his organization into one endeavor: getting France to disrupt the Olympics. He was helped by a wave of fanatical adoration for Tibet, since the mysticism of a few credit-card hippies was rivaled only by their ignorance about what life was like in Tibet under the Dalai Lamas, and what it was likely to be again if they won their battle. Drunk on folklore and anti-Chinese sentiment, several hundred troublemakers began agitating in Paris in April 2008, galvanized by firm convictions that they never even thought to cross-reference with other contradictory works by writers and journalists (a few have told what they know), reports by members of Parliament or the work of historians, sociologists, anthropologists and even Buddhologists.

In Paris that April, the disruptive element particularly appreciated the complicity of city mayor Bertrand Delanoë, who hung a banner on city hall bearing a carefully worded message: "Paris defends human rights around the world." A few days later, he made the Dalai Lama an "honorary citizen" of the city of Paris. Officials from the Green Party flew the Tibetan flag, along with a square of fabric that replaced the Olympic rings with handcuffs. Robert Ménard and a few mountain climbers hung the same black flag atop Notre Dame Cathedral and elsewhere, which was excellent for television. Commercially, RWB pulled off a sales campaign of anti-China t-shirts that ultimately brought in a million euros, as the organization trumpeted.

The Olympic torch finally began to cross Paris in the hands of closely-managed athletes. When it was the turn of a paralyzed young Chinese athlete, Jin Jing, to bear the torch in her wheelchair, crazed protesters threw themselves at her to tear it away. Despite their rush, she victoriously defended the torch, and images of the scene were broadcast around the world. Chinese television stations replayed them constantly, and appalled Chinese officials in Paris decided to interrupt the relay.

In France, it is impossible to grasp the importance of the Chinese word *mianzi*, which means "face" or "social identity." Losing *mianzi* means losing face or suffering an affront. That was how the Chinese perceived the incidents surrounding the Olympic torch in Paris.

Riding high after this success, RWB dialed up the pressure on French President Nicolas Sarkozy to boycott the Olympic Games opening ceremony and mark France as officially absent. The NGO performed a survey which showed that the majority of France now supported the boycott. President Sarkozy vacillated, postponed his decision and listened to unofficial mutterings by the Chinese saying, "He can come if he wants, but he won't be welcome." In the end, he took off on August 8 for a quick round trip: 20 hours of travel for 10 hours on site, not even one night. The French press poked fun at "speedy Sarko's sprint to Beijing."[109]

During the Parade of Nations, the enthusiastic crowd loudly applauded everyone—except for the French, who were booed.

A few days later, former prime minister Jean-Pierre Raffarin flew to Beijing to face a delicate situation in which Chinese public opinion, which traditionally has been fa-

---

109. "Le sprint de speedy Sarko à Pékin." *20 minutes,* August 5, 2008.

vorable to France ever since General de Gaulle declared his support for admitting China into the UN (instead of Taiwan), was suddenly hostile. The French Embassy in Beijing advised French nationals to practice discretion and prudence, and protesters gathered in front of French stores.

Christian Poncelet, then president of the French Senate and therefore the second-ranking state official, was also sent to Beijing, bearing soothing words and a letter of sympathy from President Sarkozy. He took care to visit Jin Jing, the athlete who had been attacked in Paris.

A few months later, in December 2008, Nicolas Sarkozy met the Dalai Lama in Gdansk, Poland, "as the EU president."[110]

France does not recognize an independent state of Tibet any more than any other country in the world. Its politicians are exhausting themselves with this shilly-shallying, which would end if they were correctly informed about the Dalai Lama's plans and how he currently uses and would later use his temporal power. In fact, they should distance themselves from those plans if they hope to protect their image as democratic representatives who believe in our Constitution. As for the French people, who have long since demonstrated their approval for the separation of church and state, if they knew the truth, they would undoubtedly withdraw their support for any sort of maneuvering whose aim is to restore a theocracy. No doubt they

---

110. AFP, December 6, 2008.

would also be shocked to know the West is financing the Dalai Lama without requiring any social improvements for the Tibetans, despite the region's serious deficiencies. Then again, admitting the need for such improvements in Tibet would force us to recognize it in our own backyard as well.

If they knew the truth, the French would also frown on the counter-productive gesticulating that produces no concrete progress and selectively aims its spite at only one among the 150 or more countries whose system we do not want in France. Curiously, that same spite is never directed at a superpower that regularly brings terror, torture, destruction and massacre to regions far outside its own borders, within which political power is handed smoothly back and forth thanks to an immense, indifferent mass of non-voters and the colossal sums of money required by anyone hoping to run for election. All of this blends together into a democratic sauce that protects the country's true credo: business is business.

7. Long Live Secular Democracy!

"We have recently embarked on changes that will further democratize and strengthen our administration in exile." [111]

How can the Dalai Lama rally international opinion to his side while the branch of Buddhism he represents remains tied to a dictatorial constitution? The task is so completely impossible that His Holiness has to sprinkle his statements liberally with the word "democracy" and make speeches demonstrating his desire to put the past behind him. Unfortunately, for those who study his texts and observe the way he treats his opponents (Shugden), it seems quite clear that his old demons are still there, simply waiting for better days.

In his speech to the European Parliament in Stras-

111. Dalai Lama's speech on "Buddhism and Democracy" given in Washington, D.C. in April 1993.

bourg on October 24, 2001, the Dalai Lama explained democracy: "This year we have taken another big stride in the process of democratization by having the chairman of the Tibetan Cabinet elected by popular vote." Yet he also added that the elected parliament and its members would limit themselves to "running Tibetan affairs," since he himself still played the main role: "However, I do consider it my moral obligation to the six million Tibetans to continue taking up the Tibetan issue with the Chinese leadership and to act as the free spokesman of the Tibetan people until a solution is reached."

For readers who remain skeptical, here are some excerpts from the charter (a program equivalent to a constitution) of the government established by the Dalai Lama in Dharamsala. I should specify that the content of this document is so unacceptable and had such a negative impact that the Dalai Lama's advocates now claim it is valid only for the period of exile, and will not be applied in Tibet. Strangely enough, it has disappeared from pro-Dalai Lama websites.

Article 3 defines the "Nature of Tibet's Polity" and explains, "The future Tibetan Polity shall uphold the principle of non-violence and shall endeavour to be a free Social welfare State with its politics guided by the Dharma."

In other words, the Dharma—a religious law—will prevail over civil law.

In article 36, the charter discusses the source of legislative power: "All legislative power and authority shall rest in the Tibetan Assembly, and such legislation shall require the assent of His Holiness the Dalai Lama to become law." So the Assembly has all the power . . . as long as His Holiness agrees! Article 19 on executive power testifies to this state of affairs:

"The executive power of the Tibetan Administration shall be vested in His Holiness the Dalai Lama, and shall be exercised by Him, either directly or through officers subordinate to Him, in accordance with the provisions of this Charter. In particular, His Holiness the Dalai Lama shall be empowered to execute the following executive powers as the chief executive of the Tibetan people.

> (a) approve and promulgate bills and regulations prescribed by the Tibetan Assembly;
>
> (b) promulgate acts and ordinances that have the force of law;
>
> (c) confer honors and patents of merit;
>
> (d) summon, adjourn, postpone and prolong the Tibetan Assembly;
>
> (e) send messages and addresses to the Tibetan Assembly whenever necessary;
>
> (f) dissolve or suspend the Tibetan Assembly;
>
> (g) dissolve the Kashag [government] or remove a Kalon or Kalons [ministers];
>
> (h) summon emergency and special meetings of major significance; and
>
> (j) authorize referendums in cases involving major issues in accordance with this Charter."

One thing is clear: the Dalai Lama is neither the head of nor a participant in the "democratic" government, but is instead above the common sphere of mortals and institutions, a self-proclaimed spokesman, living god and supreme guide.

The Charter even ends with a "special resolution," passed in 1991, which reads in part as follows: "His Holiness the Dalai Lama, the supreme leader of the Tibetan people, has given the ideals of democracy to the Tibetan people, even if he did not feel the need for such ideals. All Tibetans in Tibet and in exile are and remain deeply grateful to His Holiness the Dalai Lama, and we renew our commitment to put our faith and loyalty in His Holiness the Dalai Lama, and to pray fervently that he remain always with us as our supreme spiritual and temporal leader."

"The social life in this vast and arid country [. . .] resembles our own in the Middle Ages. The sovereignty of the clergy is firmly established here. The country's absolute monarch is also its highest religious leader, a pontiff considered to be superhuman."[112]

If there is one strong value that binds the French together, it is secularism: the separation of church and state. The Law of December 9, 1905 protects this value with its principles of reciprocal non-interference: religions must have no influence over politics, and vice-versa. A secular government guarantees freedom of religion and faith, and

112. Translated from David-Néel, Alexandra. *Mercure de France.* June 1, 1920.

makes all religious beliefs equal. In France, for example, it would have been impossible to implement the principle of secularism—a new concept allowing civil and religious power to coexist—without challenging the outrageous prerogatives the Church had amassed from its past omnipotence, which at times reached the level of political and ideological totalitarianism (with auto-da-fés, blacklisting, the Inquisition, burning at the stake, the St. Bartholomew's Day massacre, and so on). In other words, the birth of secularism erased certain religious privileges through a struggle that was viewed by the French Republic as expanding freedoms, and by the Church as persecution.

Our country respects every religion and all believers. It is not atheistic—the law protects believers against any type of discrimination—and yet secular law overrides religious precepts. The French Constitution could never be set aside in favor of other "sacred" texts.

Now, a century after the law was passed in 1905, it is rare for anyone in France to recommend restoring the Catholic religion's old privileges. Nearly unanimously, people believe that the Church should stay out of political, judicial and legislative affairs. Religions no longer have any power to interfere in state affairs, control the government or perform any political function whatsoever.

Nonetheless, a (very) small minority of people in France have adopted a somewhat irrational mindset: they treasure secularism at home, yet still dream of founding a far-off state that would abolish the principle before tearing up the country, something they would never want to see happen in France (our imprisoned separatists will understand what I mean).

The principle of secularism cannot be applied in a country where a single man, according to his religion, is vested with both spiritual and temporal power thanks to the divine privilege resulting from his miraculous birth.

In other words, it is not enough for the aging Dalai Lama, now beaten in his struggle to lead Tibet, to speak out at this late stage from Dharamsala and ask to be allowed back as a "simple monk," renouncing all his powers (although not entirely, since he intends to remain a "moral and religious leader"). The Dalai Lama's claim that he wishes for a "free, modern, secular, democratic Tibet that respects the constitution of China" does no good if, at the same time, he is organizing a theocratic government in exile that features a Department of Religion and Culture, a Council for Religious Affairs and 43 members of parliament, including two to represent each of the four Buddhist schools and two to represent the pre-Buddhist religion.

The official translation of the *Guidelines for Future Tibet's Polity and Basic Features of Its Constitution,* which His Holiness issued on 26 February 1992, announces that, "Since education is key to the development of good human beings [. . .], special attention will be paid to formulate a sound educational policy ['sound,' which some say could also mean 'just' or 'sensible']. All assistance will be given to schools, universities, institutes for science, technology and other professional trainings."

What type of education will this be? Who will dispense it, in establishments that never existed under the absolute authority of the Dalai Lamas and could blossom only after the current Dalai Lama had fled to India? The way schools are organized in the Tibetan community in exile, with mandatory prayer and portraits of the Dalai Lama in every classroom, frighteningly suggests a major step backward for education in Tibet.

The Dalai Lama's contradictions and constant reversals from one day to the next are destroying his credibility. If he hopes to be believed, he must make stronger commitments, contractualize them and dissolve his "government," an organization in which half (3 out of 6) of his cabinet are family members and other relatives hold positions at various levels in the Parliament and entities responsible for foreign affairs.

Without a doubt, the fossilized dogma of the Dalai Lama's branch of Buddhism must be updated and modernized for the 21st century; he must promise not to intervene in public education; and a critical look must be taken at Tibet under the 13 previous Dalai Lamas, and under the current one. He must accept the information and progress that has indelibly marked the world's modern societies, in which power flows (at least in theory) from the people and not from a deity. He must reject anything that could cause cultural, economic, political or social stagnation. He must admit, publicly and without reservation, that education is beneficial. And after so many years in exile and in contact with other worlds, isn't it finally time to draft a secular charter that makes no attempt to expel China's other ethnic groups and guarantees that there will be no return to limitless power for an idle, religious fraction of society? Isn't it time to come out in favor of mixed marriages (between Tibetans and other ethnic groups) and accept the existence of other religions, or the right to practice none at all?

Several of the Dalai Lama's recent statements have destabilized those who once saw him as an ocean of wisdom. Although the Dalai Lama claims to be in favor of condoms and contraception, when weekly publication *Le Point* asked him about homosexuality on March 23, 2001, he answered:

"That is part of what we Buddhists describe as 'improper sexual behavior.' The sex organs were created for reproduction between the masculine element and the feminine element, and anything that deviates from that use is unacceptable from a Buddhist perspective [counting on his fingers]: between a man and a man, a woman and another woman, in the mouth, the anus or even using the hand [miming the gesture of masturbation]."[113] When that statement triggered a heated response, he asked his spokes-

113. Translated from Gautier, François. "Sexe, morale et vache folle : le dalaï-lama parle." *Le Point*, March 23, 2001. http://www.lepoint.fr/archives/article.php/69035

persons to clarify it by explaining that Buddhism is not homophobic.

Although the man certainly has the right to change his mind and redefine his claims and decrees over the decades, years or even days, the sheer quantity of contradictory speeches is surprising and alarming.

The reality is that, even as he claims now to accept what he rejected until recently, preferring to mount an insurrection and then carry on a half-century of anti-Chinese guerilla diplomacy around the world, he is still running a "Tibetan government-in-exile" out of India, producing documents and speeches that reflect his past demands, refusing to take stock of the past, repeatedly stating his reservations about the benefits of education, and intervening to exclude from the Tibetan community-in-exile those he deems heretics, criminals or lackeys of the Chinese devils. Finally, he describes his proposal for independence as the "Middle Way" and has developed a "Charter of the Tibetans-in-Exile" which so completely fails to hide its theocratic core that he must specify it as applying only to his "kingdom" in Dharamsala, and not to Tibet.

He has made his friends insist, "The Dalai Lama does not have the questionable ambition of restoring an old and outdated regime."[114] But exactly which old and outdated

---

114. Translated from "Organisation de la communauté tibétaine en exil. Le gouvernement tibétain en exil." September 10, 2009. http://www.savetibet.fr/2009/09/organisation-de-la-communaute-tibetaine-en-exil-le-gouvernement-tibetain-en-exil/

customs or practices does he mean? He has never described them in detail. Is the regime that he plans not to restore simply too old? Is that its only failing? Obviously, he has not yet decided to repent and decry the way Tibet was under the other Dalai Lamas. His silence on this score is deafening, and leaves the door wide open for fanatics and destroyers of freedom.

"As we develop our community in exile on modern lines, we also cherish and preserve our own identity and culture and bring hope to millions of our countrymen and -women in Tibet."[115]

Are we to understand that these modern lines will be abandoned upon the Dalai Lama's hypothetical return to Tibet? Does the preservation of identity allow for mixed marriages with other Chinese ethnic groups and foreigners, or does it imply the credo of "pure race"? Are past social and political customs part of the culture being preserved?

The Dalai Lama returning to Lhasa would be like the old fairy tale wolf entering the 21st-century sheepfold, with the implicit promise of undoing everything that has been accomplished since 1959. This does not mean a return to the old feudal state, which not a single Tibetan would want today, but instead an opportunity to sit in his immense Potala Palace and call down domestic force and foreign assistance to restore his temporal rule over a vast region, along with certain privileges and old prejudices that come

---

115. Dalai Lama, Nobel Prize lecture, December 10, 1989.

with Buddhism. I believe that this is what would happen. It would lead to a global crisis, causing violent unrest that would leave China weakened and wounded, Tibet itself ravaged and Buddhism discredited as a harmful and suspect political theory, an enemy to the glorious homeland. This is the fate shared by every religion that seizes temporal power: they fall victim to it in the end. "When they dominate, they compromise their spiritual aspects; when they are dominated, they suffer the discrimination that results from the existence of an official religion."[116]

In certain trendy socio-political circles, people are blithely willing to accept a price that others will have to pay, on the principle that the ones who push are not the ones who fall.

Others, including myself, prefer to stand up for life and for the right of Buddhists to practice a religion that, since it is not a Trojan horse, is not setting itself up to be attacked either. "The Tibetan religion, however, which is suspected—not without reason—of having ties to political dissidence and 'separatism,' remains under close surveillance."[117]

We know that the entire Muslim religion is being carefully watched in North America, because one element of Islam has been linked to terrorism; it is sometimes perse-

---

116. Translated from Pena-Ruiz, Henri. *Qu'est-ce que la laïcité?* Paris, Gallimard, 2003.

117. Translation of the report by the interparliamentary friendship group of the French Senate on October 17, 2007.

cuted and often the subject of media campaigns. The recent past has taught us that, for no reason other than being Muslim, citizens of various countries have been kidnapped by the CIA, caged, humiliated, tortured, driven crazy and even murdered in the Guantanamo penal colony. The Xinjiang Uygur Autonomous Region, home to a population of Muslim Uygurs and plagued along its borders by Pakistani and Afghan fundamentalists, poses a problem in China; the NED is even developing four intervention programs for the region.

Surely all this is enough to prove, if it is not self-evident, that combining religion and government adds nothing to either, but instead destroys the serenity and credibility of both.

Who could possibly be against the right of all Chinese, in Tibet and elsewhere, to live in peace, not under an institutional status quo that accepts the current state of democracy in China, but under a system that instead strives to speed its progress (which is occurring)? Such a system would ban any attitude that might encourage Beijing's backward motion, which has already etched a negative image of China into the Western mind. This image is no caricature sketched by enemies outside the country's borders. It reflects what the country once was and still is in some aspects: the only ones our media is capable of seeing.

I sincerely hope that those who love Tibet and its culture, or simply Buddhism, will continue striving for a better relationship between the central government and this sensitive region. I hope they push for faster progress toward democracy in China, refuse to tolerate media campaigns that stir up hate based on lies that can only result in useless violence, and ultimately, succeed in creating a better world without ever being forced to subscribe to the political, economic, judicial, social or media system of the Middle Kingdom.

As you can see, although this book has absolutely no empathy for the Dalai Lama as an underhanded political leader, it is not a pamphlet against Buddhism. Rather, it laments the ways in which Buddhism has been twisted for purposes that we would be astonished (and terribly saddened) to find enshrined in an immortal sacred text.

Likewise, anyone who looks through these pages for an ode to China and the paradise of modern Tibet will do so in vain. To borrow the words of Jean-Luc Mélenchon, "I am not a Chinese communist. I never will be. But I disagree with the demonstrations calling for a boycott of the Olympic games. I disagree with Robert Ménard's campaign against the Beijing Olympics. I disagree with the rewriting of Chinese history that the campaign has produced. I absolutely do not share a blind admiration for the Dalai Lama or the regime he represents."[118]

In short, my only goal in writing this book was to promote the free practice of Buddhism, civil peace, democratic

---

118. Translated from the blog of Jean-Luc Mélenchon, http://www.jean-luc-melenchon.fr/2008/04/07/je-ne-suis-pas-daccord-avec-le-boycott-des-jeux-de-pekin-et-la-propagande-anti-chinoise/. April 7, 2008.

progress and the material and intellectual development of Tibet, which for too long has been kept alienated, stagnant and miserable by politico-religious fanaticism.

For the reasons I have stated, China will not give up the Tibet Autonomous Region in favor of a Tibet whose strings are pulled by the Dalai Lama, his sycophants and his sponsors.

Appendix A:
Historical Status of the Tibetan Autonomous Region

"Of all the changes I saw in China, those on 'the roof of the world' were the most dramatic. A leap over a thousand years from theocracy, serfdom, and slavery. . . ."

—Israel Epstein (1915-2005), *My China Eye*

China is a unified country with 56 ethnic minorities. Throughout history, a major member of this big family are the Tibetans, who have settled the Tibet Autonomous Region, most parts of Qinghai Province, southern Gansu Province, northwest Sichuan Province, and northwest Yunnan Province.

Before the unification of the Tibetan race in the 7th Century A.D., its various tribes maintained close ties with the Han Chinese and several other ethnic groups in western and northwestern China. In 629 A.D., Tubo King Songtsan Gambo unified the various Tibetan tribes on the Qinghai-Tibet Plateau and formed the Tubo Kingdom, which later maintained frequent contact with the central government of the Tang Dynasty (618-907), during what is commonly known as the "Golden Age" of dynastic China. The Tibetan-Han marriages of Songtsan Gambo to Princess Wen Cheng and Tride Zhotsan to Princess Jin Cheng, indicate that the Tibetan and the Han groups had formed close political, economic, and cultural ties. In the mid-9th century, however, the unified Tubo Kingdom collapsed. This was followed by the rise of many local warring factions in the Tibetan areas of the Qinghai-Tibet Plateau. When the Song Dynasty (960-1279) was founded in the Han-dominated areas of China, some of these local Tibetan forces (Tibetan tribes formerly under the Tubo Kingdom) pledged allegiance to the Song court, and the relationship between the Tibetan and Han grew closer during this period.

When the Mongols founded the Yuan Dynasty in the 13th Century (1271-1368), a dynasty characterized by unprecedented territorial conquest as well as ethnic unity in China, Tibet was officially incorporated into the Chinese nation. Kublai Khan, the founding emperor of the Yuan Dynasty, granted the Sagya regime the power to administer Tibet under the rule of the Yuan government. He also introduced many rules and regulations to be applied to Tibet. Thus, the Mongol, Han, Tibetan, and various other ethnicities joined together to form an incredibly diverse Chinese nation.

The Ming Dynasty (1368-1644) continued the various systems introduced during the Yuan Dynasty for dynastic administration over Tibet. In carrying out a policy of passive governance, the Ming Dynasty granted the title "Prince of Dharma" or "Prince" to eight government and religious leaders in the Tibetan area. During this period, the Tibetan areas and the central plains maintained frequent economic and cultural exchanges; the relations between the Tibetans and other Chinese ethnic groups continued to develop. By the mid-17th Century, the Ming Dynasty had collapsed and the Manchu ethnic group unified China and founded the Qing Dynasty (1644-1911), China's last imperial dynasty. The Qing government granted the honorific title "Dalai Lama" to the Dalai, and the honorary title "Panchen Erdeni" to the Panchen; it also appointed local government officials, dispatched high commissioners to Tibet, and enacted laws and regulations aimed at more effective governance of Tibet. This helped strengthen the Qing government's administration over Tibet and led to closer ties between Tibet and China which lasted until the mid 19th-century.

Throughout history, members of the Tibet noble class cherished certificates of appointment, seals of authority, and honorific titles given to them by emperors or imperial courts of the Yuan, Ming, and Qing dynasties. They held these as authenticating objects of political power. In Tibet, the Kashag (the feudal council representing the noble class) had all their statutes and documents stamped with seals issued by the imperial court to show their authority. The 5th Dalai Lama himself declared that his title and power came from the Chinese emperor.

Beginning in the mid 1800s, toward the latter part of the Qing Dynasty, China entered into a period of stagnation and decline. The reasons were brought about by both internal and external factors, including the Taiping Rebellion, the Opium Wars, and the Boxer Rebellion. Western nations subjected China to a series of humiliating military defeats, unfair treaties, and policies of extraterritoriality that would eventually lead to the collapse of China's imperial system. Not surprisingly, relations between Tibetan local government and the Chinese capital worsened.

With the China-Tibet bond weakened, nations such as Great Britain immediately recognized the strategic importance of Tibet in dealing with its interests in India, and left no stone unturned in its attempt to cultivate pro-British elements among the upper echelon of the ruling class in Tibet; the resultant Simla Conference was aimed at tearing Tibet away from China, but Tibet maintained ties with Beijing, and, even through the tumultuous war years of the 20th Century, China continued to exercise sovereignty over Tibet, as it had done since the Yuan Dynasty.

The Wuchang uprising, which began on October 10, 1911, perpetuated the beginning of the Revolution of 1911 and the official end of the Qing Dynasty. Led by Dr. Sun Yat-sen, the Republic of China was born. In less than two months following the Wuchang uprising, 14 out of

18 inland provinces declared independence from the Qing. By doing so, they distanced themselves from China's imperial rule and aligned themselves with the new Nationalist leadership; in no way did any of China's provinces seek to "declare independence" or break away from China.

In the last few decades, certain misperceptions in mainstream Western media, supported by groups led by the 14th Dalai Lama, have concocted and perpetuated a theory of "Tibetan independence," which is precariously tied to China's 1911 Revolution as Tibet's "starting over point", and which has blurred the vision of many people who are not clear about the facts of history. In recent years, Tibet has been glamorized by Hollywood actors and notable Western popular culture figures. The 14th Dalai Lama himself is a hit on the college lecture circuit and was awarded the Nobel Peace Prize in 1989, much to China's bewilderment. No one doubts the spiritual impact of the Dalai Lama on millions of people around the globe, but the facts of history should be made clear.

Contrary to popular belief, Tibet did not exist as an independent, sovereign nation that was "invaded" by China; nor was it ever a "Shangri-La" populated by free, emancipated monks living in harmony away from the outside world. In fact, the political maneuvering to bring about independence for Tibet has a history of over 100 years with four distinct stages:

1. The period from around 1910 to 1924, when pro-

British forces "stirred the pot" after the 13th Dalai Lama fled to India and later adopted the policy of "sitting on the wall to feel the wind" after having prevented a pro-British coup attempt.

2. The period from around 1934 to 1941, when the "Living Buddhas" Razheng and Dagzha came to power along with pro-Tibetan and pro-British forces, respectively.

3. The period from 1952 to 1959, when anger among reactionary elements within the Tibetan ruling class simmered, eventually leading to armed rebellion and the "tearing up" of the 1951 Agreement.

4. The period from 1960, when the armed rebellion was put down, to the present day, where the 14th Dalai Lama is now known as a global figure and media sensation after being awarded the Nobel Peace Prize in 1989.

When the former Soviet Union and former Eastern-bloc countries collapsed in the early 1990s, the Dalai clique rejoiced, hoping a similar fate would befall China. At that time, the 14th Dalai Lama predicted boldly that Tibet realize independence within five years. With the increased rise in China's national and international strength, its living standard, economy, and infrastructure, the Dalai Lama has changed is tune, claiming that Tibetan Independence won't be realized in this generation but the next; if not the next, then in the following generation, etc.

The reality is this: while it can be fairly stated that China did make mistakes in how it dealt with the Tibet issue, any notion of "Tibetan independence" is completely false. It is both theoretically and practicably impossible. The attempts to make "Tibetan independence" a reality go against all historical precedents and will not come to pass.

Seeing the CPC still provides the leadership for a prospering People's Republic of China which sees strengthened national might during the reform and opening, and the international prestige of China has increasingly risen, and national unity has been strengthened, the 14th Dalai Lama changed his tune, claiming: "Tibetan independence won't be realized in this generation. It will be realized in the next generation, if not, then in the following generation."

Soon after the liberation of China in 1949, plans were made to implement the peaceful transition of Tibet and its resultant infrastructure into the "new" People's Republic of China. Tibet was peacefully liberated in 1951 with the full cooperation of the Dalai Lama and Panchen Lama. But the core dichotomy remained: that of the newly-emerged, socialist China, and the land and serf-owning wealthy elite in Tibet. This proved to be a recipe for disaster, and in 1959, an armed revolt by the land owners precipitated a full-scale response from China, which, unfortunately, set back by decades the agreed-upon policies of reform.

Under the aegis of the Chinese government, fundamental changes have taken place in Tibet over the past six decades. Great attention has been paid to reducing illiteracy rates. Primary schools have been set up one after another in Qamdo, Lhasa, Gyangze, Xigaza, and other regions. In September 1956, the first modern middle school was founded in Lhasa, and various training and curriculum development programs were begun in order to bring Tibet into the orbit of contemporary education alongside China proper.

In old Tibet, under the feudal serf system, the vast majority of serfs and slaves struggled for existence on the verge of death, and they had no right to an education. Prior to 1951, education was primarily reserved for children of the noble class and there were no modern schools, with mass illiteracy (90%) the norm. The notion of "religious freedom" in old Tibet is a myth. Impoverished young monks and nuns, after entering monasteries or nunneries, spent their days performing hard labor and menial tasks, suffering untold misery for years. Beaten and abused, they became monastic slaves. They had no time to take part in real religious activities. Among the vast numbers of monks and nuns in old Tibet, many were forced into monastic life. The elite often played once sect against the other, even relying on one sect to act against opposing sects. The so-called "heyday" of religion in Tibet was based upon the sufferings of the majority and the oppression and exploitation of farmers, herders, monks and nuns.

In China, citizens enjoy the freedom of religious belief stipulated in the Chinese Constitution and state laws, and also bear duties laid down by the Constitution and laws. The Chinese Constitution clearly stipulates that no one shall use religion to sabotage social order, damage the physical and mentally health of its citizens, curb the state educational system, or interfere in the administration of justice. The abolished feudal religious privilege or the systems of oppression and exploitation will not be allowed to recover, nor will any sabotage of state unification and national unity be permitted. Religious people who use religion to engage in illegal or criminal activities and those who hold no religious belief but have committed crimes will all be punished according to the law. From 1987 to 1989, a handful of separatists incited riots in Lhasa. Among these were lamas and nuns, as well as the common masses. They attempted to overthrow the state's political power.

Respecting and protecting the freedom of religious belief is a fundamental policy of the Chinese Government. This basic policy means: every Chinese citizen has the freedom to believe or not to believe in religion; has the freedom to believe in the established religion of their choice and enjoys the freedom to follow the sect of their choice, the freedom to change religious beliefs, adopting beliefs not formerly held, or abandoning former beliefs. The essence of this basic policy is to give every Chinese citizen the freedom to choose his or her own faith in regard to religious beliefs and to make religious belief a private matter of each citizen. The Central Government has implemented this policy in Tibet. The overall implementation of the policy of freedom of religious belief in Tibet has gained sincere support from the people of religious circles, and equally from those who do not believe in any religion.

The beliefs of more than 100,000 overseas Tibetans are also constantly changing. Those who harbored serious separatist tendencies in the past and later bore the bumps and bruises of the road towards "Tibetan independence" have learned lessons from their own bitter and sad experiences. One ethnic Kamba who used to be responsible for relations with the Taiwan authorities stated in 1985: "The plot of the 'government-in-exile' has been disclosed. It is clear that 'Tibetan independence' is impossible. We were cheated in the past, and should work exclusively for our future livelihood."[119]

119. Su, Shuyang. *A Tibet Reader*. Foreign Languages Press, 2009

APPENDIX B:
List of the Dalai Lamas

First Dalai Lama: Gedun Drup (1391-1474)

Second Dalai Lama: Gendun Gyatso (1475-1542)

Third Dalai Lama: Sonam Gyatso (1543-1588)

Fourth Dalai Lama: Yonten Gyatso (1589-1616)

Fifth Dalai Lama: Ngawang Lozang Gyatso (1617-1682)

Sixth Dalai Lama: Tsangyang Gyatso (1683-1706)

Seventh Dalai Lama: Kelzang Gyatso (1708-1757)

Eighth Dalai Lama: Jampel Gyatso (1758-1804)

Ninth Dalai Lama: Lungtok Gyatso (1805-1815)

Tenth Dalai Lama: Tsultrim Gyatso (1816-1837)

Eleventh Dalai Lama: Khedrup Gyatso (1838-1855)

Twelfth Dalai Lama: Trinley Gyatso (1856-1875)

Thirteenth Dalai Lama: Thuben Gyatso (1876-1933)

Fourteenth Dalai Lama: Tenzin Gyatso (1935-   )

Bibliography

Dalai Lama:

My Land and My People, The Original Autobiography of His Holiness the Dalai Lama of Tibet. New York, McGraw-Hill, 1962.

Liberté pour le Tibet. Message de paix et de tolérance. Paris, L'Arganier, 2008.

Nobel Prize acceptance speech and lecture, December 10, 1989.

Charter of the Tibetans-in-Exile, June 14, 1991.

Official translation of the Guidelines for Future Tibet's Polity and Basic Features of Its Constitution, which His Holiness issued on February 26, 1992.

Speech on "Buddhism and Democracy," Washington, D.C., April 1993.

Speech to the European Parliament, Strasbourg, October 24, 2001.

Speech on the 49th Anniversary of the Tibetan National Uprising Day, Dharamsala, March 10, 2008.

Other authors:

Aron, Raymond. Memoirs: Fifty Years of Political Reflection. Holmes and Meier, 1990.

David-Néel, Alexandra, Grand Tibet et vaste Chine. Paris. Omnibus 1994, republished 1999.

Epstein, Israel, *My China Eye*: Memoirs of a Jew and a Journalist. Long River Press, 2005.

Ménard, Robert. Des libertés et autres chinoiseries. Paris, Robert Laffont, 2008.

Nicol, Mike. Compassion: The Words and Inspiration of the Dalai Lama, preface by Desmond Tutu. Hachette Livre Australia, 2008.

Su, Shuyang, *A Tibet Reader*. Foreign Languages Press, 2009.

Vivas, Maxime. La Face cachée de Reporters sans frontières. De la CIA aux faucons du Pentagone, Paris, Aden, 2007.

Report by the Franco-Tibetan friendship group to the French Senate, June 14, 2006.

Report by the interparliamentary friendship group of the French Senate, October 17, 2007.

France 24, Report on August 9, 2008.

National Endowment for Democracy, website, January 2011.

International Centre for Prison Studies, King's College London.

And also:

Reporters Without Borders, Amnesty International, France-Tibet, Tibet-Info, AFP, Der Spiegel, Libération, France Culture, Le Point, Los Angeles Times, Le Monde diplomatique, Washington Post, New York Times.

32834701R00085

Made in the USA
San Bernardino, CA
17 April 2019